Empathic Teaching
Promoting Social Justice in the Contemporary Classroom

Nicholas D. Young
Elizabeth Jean
Teresa A. Citro

Series in Education

VERNON PRESS

Copyright © 2019 Vernon Press, an imprint of Vernon Art and Science Inc, on behalf of the author.

All rights reserved. No part of this publication may be reproduced, stored in a retrieval system, or transmitted in any form or by any means, electronic, mechanical, photocopying, recording, or otherwise, without the prior permission of Vernon Art and Science Inc.

www.vernonpress.com

In the Americas:
Vernon Press
1000 N West Street,
Suite 1200, Wilmington,
Delaware 19801
United States

In the rest of the world:
Vernon Press
C/Sancti Espiritu 17,
Malaga, 29006
Spain

Series in Education

Library of Congress Control Number: 2019931227

ISBN: 978-1-62273-715-4

Also available:

Hardback: 978-1-62273-615-7

E-book: 978-1-62273-642-3

Product and company names mentioned in this work are the trademarks of their respective owners. While every care has been taken in preparing this work, neither the authors nor Vernon Art and Science Inc. may be held responsible for any loss or damage caused or alleged to be caused directly or indirectly by the information contained in it.

Every effort has been made to trace all copyright holders, but if any have been inadvertently overlooked the publisher will be pleased to include any necessary credits in any subsequent reprint or edition.

Cover design by Vernon Press, using elements designed by Pressfoto / Freepik.

Table of Contents

Acknowledgement v

Preface vii

Chapter One
The Leaders of Equity: Past and Present 1
   Elizabeth Jean, *Endicott College*
   Anne E. Mead, *Danbury Public Schools*

Chapter Two
**Fostering Growth in the Classroom: Climate,
Culture and Supports that Make a Difference** 13
   Elizabeth Jean, *Endicott College*
   Gena Rotas, East *Longmeadow, MA*

Chapter Three
**Academic and Social Success Cycles: Promoting
Socially Just Classroom Experiences for ALL Students** 31
   Jacqueline Hawkins, *University of Houston*
   Sara J. Jones, *University of Houston*
   Kristi L. Santi, *University of Houston*

Chapter Four
**All Money Matters: Socioeconomic
Factors and the Impact on Learning** 47
   Dariel T. Henry,
   Massasoit Community College and Regis College

Chapter Five
**Religious Practices in the Classroom:
Understanding and Honoring the Differences** 61
   Nicholas D. Young, *American International College*
   Haley Scott, *American International College*

Chapter Six
**Diverse Ability Levels: Differentiating Instruction to
Teach to All Learners**   75
  Jacqueline Hawkins, *University of Houston*
  Sara J. Jones, *University of Houston*
  Kristi L. Santi, *University of Houston*

Chapter Seven
**Social Justice Curricula: Design and
Implementation Across the Content Areas**   87
  Nicholas D. Young, *American International College*
  Ashley Adamski, *American International College*

Chapter Eight
**Student Leadership: A Necessary
Component in Equity Education**   99
  Nicholas D. Young, *American International College*
  Aimee Dalenta, *Goodwin College*

Chapter Nine
**Extracurricular Activities:
Promoting Equity Outside the Classroom**   111
  Micheline S. Malow, *Manhattanville College*

Chapter Ten
**Collaboration and Self-Development:
Professional Learning to Reduce Bias**   123
  Nicholas D. Young, *American International College*
  Elizabeth Jean, *Endicott College*

About the Primary Authors   135

Acknowledgement

This book would not be complete without a sincere 'thank you' to Sue Clark for her suggestions and edits, which have made this book far stronger. She is a valued member of our writing team and a wonderful person and friend. We will be forever grateful for her tremendously positive contributions to this book and to our lives.

Preface

Empathic Teaching: Promoting Social Justice in the Contemporary Classroom was written for pre-service and veteran teachers, school and educational psychologists, related special education service professionals, educational administrators, guidance counselors, graduate education professors, policy-makers, parents and student leaders. While this tome will largely focus on understanding the role that equity should play in P-12 education, it will do so with an acute awareness that there are myriad factors that influence student engagement and the motivation to learn. Although some of the subjects under consideration have been written about elsewhere broadly, this tome will offer a unique contribution by examining each from a social equity perspective. As schools move to ensure a more inclusive and well-rounded student body, this book will be a substantial asset to anyone interested in advancing a social justice agenda.

The motivation for writing this book arose due to…

- Our concern that the inequities that currently exist in schools threaten the ability of teachers and students to adequately prepare for a future that is socially just;
- Our knowledge that each administrator, educator, parent, and student play an integral part in creating schools and classrooms in which everyone feels safe, respected, and important;
- Our belief in equitable outcomes for all students so that they can become leaders of their communities and productive member of society; and
- Our passion for helping to guide the conversation surrounding social justice through research and examples, explicitly teaching the concepts that will carry the message to all who engage in raising the next generation.

Each chapter provides the reader with a better understanding of how to bring social justice concepts into the classroom and beyond. The book begins with a look at the beginnings of social justice and considers the contribution of Paulo Freire, Martin Luther King, Jr., and other influencers and continues on to explain the need for an inclusive and calm classroom culture that values all students. Engaging students in social success cycles and differentiated instruction based on a social justice curriculum promotes positive experiences in school, while an examination of extracurricular activities is also considered in this tome. Money and religion are two divisive areas and they are both considered here in terms of concerns and promising practices. Parents and students will enjoy reading about student leadership and the possibilities that exist if the student is willing, while educators and those who are involved with the schools in any fashion should consider learning more about self-development.

Written by a team of educators and professors whose life experiences and research interests span the collective concerns of equity in education, it is with confidence that we share this book with the readers. *Empathic Teaching: Promoting Social Justice in the Contemporary Classroom* is for those who are committed to using social justice as a lens through which all students can succeed in the classroom. Our overarching goal for this work is simple: We wish to support our colleagues with educating the next generation to demonstrate tolerance, respect and empathy for all others in society as a lifelong endeavor. And last, but far from least, thank you for you doing your part to achieve those same outcomes.

Chapter One

The Leaders of Equity: Past and Present

Elizabeth Jean, *Endicott College*

Anne E. Mead, *Danbury Public Schools*

The education system is plagued with inequities; both in the way it is structured and the way it is financed (Drover, 2009). Beginning in the late 1800s, the one-room schoolhouse disappeared, making room for neighborhood schools whose academics were determined by a group of neighborhood individuals known as a board of education (Church, 2015). These neighborhood schools were typically financed by the local government based on the population and housing practices (Irving, 2014, Drover, 2009). Since many communities sought to fund their systems by the local property tax, it predominantly became white communities that had the most funding, best teachers and students who could achieve (Irving, 2014).

Communities in redlined areas became schools for children of families that struggled financially, were oppressed, and often drew teachers who couldn't make it in the better suburban schools (Irving, 2014). It quickly became evident that students in these schools suffered from inadequate resources, poor quality teachers, and the beginning of systemic inequities (Drover, 2009). The evidence was clear that a division between those who could afford and those who could not attend schools with very different characteristics; a classroom that espoused cultural and education behaviors of white middle-class families at the sacrifice of less dominating and influential social classes (Irving, 2014). These inequities prompted educators to quickly switch their teaching pedagogy from a classroom focus to one that looked at systemic inequities and a society where oppressiveness is prevalent (Drover, 2009).

Paulo Freire

Defined by Freire (1970/2002), an oppressed society (those within the redlined areas) must seek out humanitarians who will free those in the affected areas. At this point in time, Freire (1970/2002) felt that those who lived in oppressed systems were aware of their living situations but did not see a way out of the oppression; rather "their perception of themselves as oppressed is impaired by their submersion in the reality of oppression" (Freire, 2002, n.p.). The oppressed were not energized, nor did they know how to overcome this level of subjugation and, thus, stayed in it longer than they should (Davis & Steyn, 2012). Outside forces would then notice the situation and try to make changes for the system (Davis & Steyn, 2012). These outside forces often included the oppressor; that is, those who were termed privileged as well as "white people who benefit from systemic whiteness" (Davis & Steyn, 2012, p. 30).

Though most of Freire's work was done in the 70s, at least one of his books stressed the need for democracy (Freire, 1985). Freire (1985) maintained that oppressed societies had the need to organize themselves to be active proponents of their own ideas and goals through education. It was argued that through political determination a democracy could be formed that ultimately developed a society of people with the characteristics of good citizens (Westheimer & Kahne, 2004). Shanker and G. W. Bush (as cited in Westheimer & Kahne, 2004) continued the cause by promoting the establishment of programs in schools that aimed to renew the democratic spirit; however, through these discussions the definition of democracy can still be unclear as it relates to students who become good citizens educated in safe schools.

The idea of safe schools was further challenged by Davis and Steyn (2012) who asked, "safe from what or whom?" (p. 33). Still today, the ideas of safe schools are not well defined. Most consider a safe school to be free of violence; however, there are often minimal discussions about how to make classrooms feel safe for students regarding issues that affect them such as LGBTQ+, cultural differences, or education inequities (Young, Michael, & Smolinski, 2019a). Safe schools must also include open discussions between the school and community regarding what equity in education means and how cultural competencies and other relevant issues can be addressed (Lopez, Patrick, & Sturgis, 2017). These discussions are just beginning.

There have been many leaders, both educational and non-educational, who have acted upon their beliefs in order to change the culture of social justice. Leaders such as Ghandi, Mandela, Martin Luther King, Jr. have had "a vision of transformative change for his or her country" (Redford, 2017, p. 1831). This led to deep-seated changes in the lives of those previously affected by marginalization and poverty. In doing so, these progressive social justice warriors created change to "laws, systems and structures that allow and create injustices" (Redford, 2017, p. 1832).

Social justice leaders are the catalyst for constructing power and changing communities that have suffered or been soundless by current situations (Redford, 2017; Capper & Young, 2014). Superintendents as social justice leaders differ from principals as they have the capacity to make large-scale systemic, transformative changes to cultural values, foundations and practices that address marginalized students (DeMatthews, Izquierdo, & Knight, 2017).

Capper and Young (2014) defined socially just educational leadership as the ability to have an inclusive culture that supports five pillars to include (1) what inclusive practice means; (2) how student achievement is accentuated; (3) the absence of policies and procedures that guide decision-making; (4) how superheroes are distinguished from collaborative leadership; and "the intersection of identity and difference" (Capper & Young, 2014, p. 158).

Martin Luther King Jr.

Martin Luther King, Jr. contributed to social justice by helping to define integration and inclusion (May, 2017). Ogletree (2004) suggested that instead of using inclusion to mean all people, that a new community should be formed where there is an improved level of tolerance and respect. Dr. King further defined the term integration as "genuine, intergroup, interpersonal doing and the ultimate goal of our national community" (Capper & Young, 2014, p. 159). This definition leaves out inclusion as a solitary term for those who are marginalized or have disabilities (Horsford, 2014). The dissection of terms also leaves behind an ill-fated definition for those with disabilities, those from lower-income families, those who experience homelessness or students who define themselves such as lesbian, gay, bisexual or transgender (Capper & Young, 2014; Horsford, 2014).

Dr. King learned about racism during his student days (The King Center, 2018; May, 2017). While not ascribing to either political party, believing that they both had weaknesses and neither promoted racial equity, Dr. King did support the work of Mohandas "Mahatna" Ghandi for his non-violence approach (May, 2017). In 1964, when DR. KING received the Nobel Peace Prize, he honored the work of Ghandi for having a "successful precedent of using non-violence to challenge the British Empire" (Carson, Armstrong, Carson, Clay, & Taylor, 2005). Ghandi and Dr. King had read several of the same books, which resulted in similar belief systems (May,

2017). Dr. King was also a follower of Thoreau's essay on Civil Disobedience (Brownlee, 2013).

Dr. King's assassination brought light to the need for discussions surrounding making meaning of the civil rights movement of the twentieth century and to begin social change around healing oppression (Ginwright, 2015). Lengthy conversations ensured that oppression turnaround was woven into the fabric of our country and that long-lasting changes were possible (Ginwright, 2015). Today, however, a "lack of organizing infrastructure; fragmentation and isolation and; lack of meaning and hope" (Ginwright, 2015, p. 36) threaten many of the critical issues facing black youth.

These issues also envelop poverty, underfunded schools, jail time, poor health care, and housing opportunities. Lee (2014) advocated that the needed changes require how our communities deal with social trauma by working on healing, transformation, and "fostering a sense of well-being" (Ginwright, 2015, p. 38). Groups using a grassroots approach are beginning to see traction in their respective areas of the country through restoration, resistance, and reclamation (Lee 2014). Further discussions need to be held countrywide in an effort to transform how communities are dealing with racial healing (Ginwright, 2015; Horsford, 2014).

Malcolm X, Mahatma Ghandi, Marian Wright Edelman and Robert Moses

Leaders such as Malcolm X and Gandhi all supported social justice changes; however, they were not as effective as current transformation initiatives are today. Two such contemporary leaders that have been more effective in changing classroom and community practices are Marian Wright Edelman and Robert Moses. Marian Wright Edelman, a policy maker from the Children's Defense Fund, has used Freedom Schools as an avenue to makes changes at the school level (Children's Defense Fund, 2018). Wright Edelman's focus on classroom literacy and educational enrichment in communities that suffer from racial injustices has been attributed to changing communities through a deep-rooted conversation on racial inequities and practices that will change the outcomes of its students (Children's Defense Fund, 2018). Robert Moses profoundly believed in King's work and developed the Algebra project that put the responsibility back into the classroom for revolutionary change (Duke University Libraries, n.d.). Using knowledge, character and action, both Wright Edelman and Moses are well known for effective changes in classrooms.

Dolores Huerta, Muhammad Ali, and Kimberly Bryant

Other social activists include Muhammad Ali who supported justice and peace from an early age, beginning with a stand against the Vietnam War, and later in life advocating for peace by being awarded the Presidential Medal of Peace in 2005 (Eig, 2017). Another Presidential Medal of Peace awardee in 2012 was Dolores Huerta. Huerta of Mexican descent, later joined by Chavez in 1962, advocated for better working conditions for farm workers (Forman, 2018). Schooled in California, Huerta quickly became aware of the inequities around income, workers' rights and conditions, and education. Advocating for education became her platform as Huerta became one of the most influential spokeswomen for labor issues in the late 90s and a leader "in the Chicano civil rights movement" (Michals, 2015). As a classroom teacher in the 1950s, Huerta witnessed firsthand the high rate of students of color suspended and expelled from school as compared to their white peers and realized this to be a significant problem (Michals, 2015).

Huerta realized that history curriculum for middle and high school was devoid of the sacrifice and the influences and contributions of people of color (Forman, 2018). Being aware of these inequities, Huerta advocated for progressives to run for local and state positions as a way to bring change to issues including personal rights, fairness, and a good education (Forman, 2018). In 1962 she founded the Agricultural Workers Association and later, with Cesar Chavez, founded the National Farm Workers Association; three years later they formed the United Farm Workers' Union with Huerta as vice president (Michals, 2015). This organization fought for health care rights and better working conditions. In 2015 she founded the Dolores Huerta Foundation that supports workers' rights, education, and family life (Michals, 2015).

Today Huerta advocates for immigrants' rights to come to the U.S. and asks for Americans to recognize the excess and wastefulness of those in Fortune 500 companies (Michals, 2015). Huerta has been vocal in pointing out America's lack of sensitivity to the homeless and those who work two or three jobs to support their families, recognizing how technology is taking jobs away for lower-income families, and has "decried the U.S. tax plan that decreases the corporate tax rate at the expenses of social equities" (Foreman, 2018, p. 4). Huerta continues to advocate for grassroots efforts at the school and community level to deal with educational inequities (Michals, 2015).

Kimberly Bryant, like Huerta, supports young girls and their ability to learn in a male-dominated world (Black Girls Code, 2018). Bryant began Black Girls Code (2018), an organization that is passionate about every young girl's ability to learn coding and technology (Black Girls Code, 2018). Based on her upbringing in Memphis she resolved that she would not be the only African-American in college studying engineering. Based on her personal experience, Black Girls Code (2018) encouraged other female individuals who felt marginalized in the classroom to remove roadblocks and be an active and accepted voice in a male-driven area of study.

Bryan Stevenson

Bryan Stevenson, founder of the Equal Justice Initiative in Montgomery, Alabama due to his belief in "fighting poverty and challenging racial discrimination in the criminal justice system" (Equal Justice Initiative, 2017, n.p.). Stevenson and the Equal Justice Initiative were convinced that rulings such as mandatory life without parole were unconstitutional for students under the age of 17 (Equal Justice Initiative, 2017). Stevenson led many ventures that helped educational communities become knowledgeable about slavery and racial segregation and his contributions led to many more students of color staying in school and being educated (Equal Justice Initiative, 2017).

Stevenson's 2014 book discussed the U.S. prison system and the outcomes of the millions of people incarcerated with the hopes of helping citizens recognize the shortcomings of the prison system, how people are treated, and the outcomes of those who had been released from prison. Stevenson (2014) advocated for children born into families who have relatives or parents incarcerated, those who were born into family violence, communities that perpetuate violence, and the poor condition of schools that continue this lifestyle. With a strong belief that schools are becoming more like prisons, with students as the inmates and educators and administrators as the leadership, Stevenson (2014) suggested that schools in which kindness was the expectation and teachers engaged with students in positive ways, offered more potential to change the narrative.

Stevenson (2014) felt that the U.S. education system needed total revamping - one that does not use the statistics from the Bureau of Justice to forecast how many males will be incarcerated; rather, it discusses the problem and finds a resolution that impacts graduation rates. Teachers must develop healthy relationships with their students and encourage problem-solving in an unjust world; yet, Stevenson (2014) realized that there was no single prescription for all schools (CEHD, 2017).

Listening to students, embracing their ideals for the future, and the willingness to break down barriers will best benefit changes to the education system, in addition to discussing the injustices of the past including wars, civil unrest, and histories that still influence today's unfortunate events (Stevenson, 2014). Changing the narrative regarding race will only occur if it is verbalized, dismantled and reimaged. Communities and educational institutions must be bold when discussing the issues and making new sense of it as a means of moving forward (Stevenson, 2014). Stevenson hopes to be able to change what is being taught, facilitating the uncomfortable discussions about race and equity, and what skills they are building in their students that will "be witness to something better, something transformative, some that moves us to a better place" (CEHD, 2017, p. 6).

Astrid Silva and Chad Griffin

Well before the Every Student Succeeds Act, educators were mindful of teaching using a social justice lens; yet, they were shaken to find out that the No Child Left Behind act required scientific-based interventions (Klein, 2015; Klein, 2016). When the federal legislation was enacted, however, teachers were still unclear as to the definition, context, and assessment to be used in a socially just teaching environment (Drover, 2009). Unfortunately, for some schools, this remains a problem as many of the scientific-based interventions use a one size fits all approach that does not accurately assess some students (Drover, 2009). Two current activists have been instrumental in making changes for individuals who may be perceived as out of the normal mainstream of America.

Astrid Silva's stance on immigration issues formed her views on education. Having been silent most of her life in an effort to avoid being uncovered as an undocumented student with a family that came to the U.S. when she was four, Silva became known as an activist in the formation of and passage of the DREAM Act (Johnson, 2016). The Act allowed those who came to the U.S. before the age of sixteen to receive legal residency, gain work permits, and avoid deportation (Johnson, 2016). After many years of being undefined or living in the shadows in the U.S., she began to advocate for herself. Today, she remains the organizing director of the Progressive Leadership Alliance of Nevada (Johnson, 2016).

Chad Griffin fights for the rights of those who are LGBTQ+ (Lesbian, Gay, Bisexual, Trans*, Queer; while the '+' indicates additional identities) through his continued engagement with the Human Rights Campaign [HRC] (HRC, 2018). With nearly three million members, the HRC was credited with the removal of Pat McCrory from North Carolina on the discriminatory HB2 legislation (HRC, 2018). Previously responsible for challenging Proposition 8, Griffin led the American Foundation for Equal Rights through an education campaign that focused on "renewable energy, land conservation, stem cell research, early childhood education, antitobacco and marriage equity" (HRC, 2018, n.p.). Griffin continues to lead communities through thought-provoking discussions to change the way LGBTQ+ policies and legislation can be integrated into communities and schools (HRC, 2018).

Final Thoughts

Although the educational systems of modern-day America may be flawed and in need of revamping, infusing social justice into all aspects of the school can only help reduce inequities. Redlined communities were those that were poverty-ridden, had inadequate resources, and poor quality teachers; whereas, white middle-class neighborhoods in which more tax money went to the schools, were able to provide a better, smarter teacher. This dichotomy produced an inequity in education of grand proportions.

A look at social justice leaders, both past and present, provides an opportunity to see the country, and thereby the schools, change in meaningful ways. Freire, Ghandi, Mandela, Martin Luther King, Jr., and so many others contributed to the social justice platform and paved the way for students and teachers to make the classroom a safer space for all.

Points to Remember

- *Paulo Freire, Martin Luther King, Jr. and others believed in a democratic society in which people modeled positive citizenship for others. Each leader had a similar platform, yet each delivered it in a different manner.*
- *Edelman and Moses were able to make substantial changes within the classroom through their creation of the Children's' Defense Fund and the Alegra Project, respectively.*
- *Huerta advocated for equitable education after seeing the inequity in the labor field. The Dolores Huerta Foundation supports education, workers' rights, and family life. Together with Chavez, the two also formed the United Farm Workers' Union.*
- *The Equal Justice Initiative, created by Bryan Stevenson, fights poverty, challenges racial discrimination, and examines the school to prison pipeline. He believes in having the difficult conversations that surround race and equity.*
- *Chad Griffin fights for the rights of the LGBTQ+ community through his work with non-profit organizations such as the Human Rights Campaign and the American Foundation for Equal Rights.*

References

Black Girls Code. (2018). *About our Founder.* Retrieved from http://www.blackgirlscode.com/about-bgc.html

Brownlee, K. (2013). *Civil Disobedience.* E.N. Zalta (ed.). Retrieved from https://plato.stanford.edu/entries/civil-disobedience/

Bryant, K. (2017). Electronic recording—Making Waves. Retrieved from www.makingways.co/episodes/kimberlybryant/

Capper, C. A & Young, M. D. (2014). Ironies and limitations of educational leadership for social justice: A call to social justice educators. Theory into Practice, 53(2), 158-164, DOI:10.1080/00405841.2014.885814

Carson, C., Armstrong, T., Carson, S., Clay, A., & Taylor, K. (eds.) (2005). *The papers of Martin Luther King, Jr.: Volume V: Threshold of a new Decade-January 1959-December 1960.* CA: University of California Press

Children's Defense Fund. (2018). *2018 fast facts.* Retrieved from https://www.childrensdefense.org/programs/cdf-freedom-schools/

Church, D. (2015). Exploring the history of one-room schoolhouses. *Hartford Courant.* Retrieved from https://www.courant.com/community/south-windsor/rnw-sw-south-windsor-one-room-schoolhouse-0625-20150616-story.html

College of Education and Human Development. (2017). Interview: Just mercy author Bryan Stevenson advocates social justice at CEHD reads event. *Regents of the University of Minnesota.* Retrieved from https://cehdvision2020.umn.edu/blog/interview-author-bryan-stevenson-cehd-reads/

Davis, D. & Steyn, M. (2012). Teaching for social justice: Reframing some pedagogical assumptions. *Perspectives in Education, 30*(4), 29-38. Retrieved from https://eric.ed.gov/?id=EJ998110

DeMatthews, D., Izquierdo, E. & Knight, D.S. (2017). Righting past wrongs: A superintendent's social justice leadership for dual language education along the U.S.-Mexico border. *Education Policy Analysis Archives, 25*(1), 1-32. Retrieved from https://files.eric.ed.gov/fulltext/EJ1126859.pdf

Drover, A. G. (2009). Teaching for social justice and K-12 student outcomes: A conceptual framework and research review. *Equity & Excellence in Education, 42*(4), 5-7-525, DOI: 10.1080/10665680903196339

Duke University Libraries. (n.d.). *Bob Moses begins algebra project.* Retrieved from https://snccdigital.org/events/bob-moses-begins-algebra-project/

Eig, J. (2017). *Ali: A Life.* New York, NY: Houghton Mifflin Harcourt.

Equal Justice Initiative. (2017). *Bryan Stevenson.* Retrieved from https://eji.org/bryan-stevenson

Foreman, H. (2018). Dolores Huerta talks education, social inequality and the new tax plan, *The Stanford Daily,* Retrieved from www.stanforddaily.com/2018/01/12/dolores-huerta-talks-education-social-inequality-and-the-new-tax-plan

Freire, P. (1985). *The politics of education: Culture, power, & liberation.* Westport, CT: Bergin & Garvey Publishers

Friere, P. (2005). Pedagogy of the Oppressed: 30th anniversary edition. New York, NY: Continuum International Publishing Group. Retrieved from http://commons.princeton.edu/inclusivepedagogy/wp-content/uploads/sites/17/2016/07/freire_pedagogy_of_the_oppresed_ch2-3.pdf

Ginswright, S. A. (2015). Radically healing black lives: A love note to justice. *New Directions for Student Leadership, 148*, 33-44. DOI: 10.1002/yd.20151

Hornsford, S. D. (2014). When race enters the room: Improving leadership and learning through racial literacy, *Theory into Practice, 53*(2), 123-130, DOI:10.1080/00405841.2014.885812

Human Rights Campaign [HRC]. (n.d.). *The HRC Story: Chad Griffin*. Retrieved from www.hrc.org/hrc-story/staff/chad-griffin1

Irving, D. (2014). *Waking up white, and finding myself in the story of race.* Cambridge, MA: Elephant Room Press

Johnson, B. (2016). *Who is Astrid Silva? Why is she speaking about immigration the DNC 2016.* Retrieved from www.nj.com/politics/index.ssf/2016/07/who_is_astrid_silva_one_of_the_day_1_speakers_at_dnc_2016.html

Klein, A. (2015). *No child left behind: An overview.* Retrieved from https://www.edweek.org/ew/section/multimedia/no-child-left-behind-overview-definition-summary.html

Klein, A. (2016). *The every student succeeds act: An ESSA overview.* Retrieved from https://www.edweek.org/ew/issues/every-student-succeeds-act/index.html

Lee, N. (2014). *Healing-centered youth organizing: A framework for youth leadership in the 21st century.* Retrieved from https://urbanpeacemovement.org/wp-content/uploads/2014/02/ConceptPaperFINALPDF.pdf

Lopez, N., Patrick, S. & Sturgis, C. (2017). Quality and equity by design: charting the course for the next phase of competency-based education. Retrieved from www.nmefoundation.org/getmedia/ecdb1d44-6c28-46fc-ab35-9d1ea64d9dd4/CompetencyWorks-QualityAndEquityByDesign?ext=.pdf

May, A. (2017). *Dr. Martin Luther King, Jr.'s evolution as an activist.* Retrieved from https://scholar.colorado.edu/cgi/viewcontent.cgi?article=2490&context=honr_theses

Michals, D. (2015). Dolores Huerta. *National Women's History Museum.* Retrieved from https://www.womenshistory.org/education-resources/biographies/dolores-huerta

Ogletree, Jr., Charles J. (2004). *All Deliberate Speed: Reflections on the First Half Century of Brown v. Board of Education.* New York, NY: W.W. Norton & Co.

Redford, K. (2017). Attention, law students: our country and your planet need you to lead, *Stanford Law Review, 69,* 1831-1840. Retrieved from https://heinonline.org/HOL/LandingPage?handle=hein.journals/stflr69&div=55&id=&page=

Stevenson, B. (2014). *Just Mercy: A story of justice and redemption.* New York, NY: Spiegel & Grau

The King Center. (2018). *About Dr. King.* Retrieved from http://www.thekingcenter.org/about-dr-king

Westheimer, J. & Kahne, J. (2004). Educating the "good" citizen: Political choices and pedagogical goals. *PS: Political Sciences & Politics, 37*(2), 241-247, DOI: 10.1017/S1049096504004160

Young, N.D., Michael, C.N., & Smolinski, J.A. (2019a). *Securing the schoolyard: Protocols that promote safety and positive student behaviors.* Lanham, MD: Roman & Littlefield.

Young, N.D., Michael, C.N., & Smolinski, J.A. (2019b). *Sounding the alarm in the schoolhouse: Safety, security, and well-being.* Lanham, MD: Roman & Littlefield.

Chapter Two

Fostering Growth in the Classroom: Climate, Culture and Supports that Make a Difference

Elizabeth Jean, *Endicott College*

Gena Rotas, East *Longmeadow, MA*

It is not by accident that the climate of the classroom reflects the values, ethics, and morals of the teacher. Designing and initiating a classroom climate for learning takes a powerful commitment to what works best for the children engaged in the space provided for gathering (Barr, 2016; Hannah, 2013). An empathic teacher knows that positive regard, positive rapport, and the ability to compassionately attune to others lays the foundation for a climate that will support success (Hannah, 2013).

On a professional and personal level, the teacher is aware and vigilant of a personal inner flow of energy and how it might impact students in the room. Based on the latest brain research, as social beings, our brains talk to each other without saying a word (HeartMath, n.d.; Bambaeeroo & Shokpour, 2017). We might consider the flow of energy as 'non-verbal communication,' yet the science goes much further. Actual brain synapse and heart rate variables are affected by just being in the presence of another human being. When the teacher is clear about unconditional acceptance, kind and respectful in attitude, has an easy and relaxed manner, can display a forgiving as well as an encouraging inclination, demonstrates an interactive and interested stance, secures and upholds a sense of safety throughout the proceedings in the classroom, then the infrastructure fosters real growth and certainly makes a significant impact on the climate in the classroom and the possibility for unequivocal learning (Bambaeeroo & Shokpour, 2017; Barr, 2016).

The attitude of the teacher is pivotal and influential to the design and construction of the climate best suited for instruction (Lee, 2011). Once the environment is secure and reliable, teaching social justice becomes an intriguing and integral part of everyday life in the classroom. The physical presentation of the classroom becomes one of cooperation, interest, participation and design contributed by all those engaged in learning (Lee, 2011).

The physical space has an impact on the climate of the classroom. Keeping in mind that children work best when there is order and predictability around them, a clean, neat, comfortable, inviting space says more than a row of desks (Hannah, 2013). Think of the furniture arrangement in a comfortable home. Where do guests sit and how do they interact with each other? What helps conversation and sharing ideas happen in a fluid manner? How do guests display comfort and ease in your space? What might some of the comments be if guests are relaxed and well taken care of by the attending host? In some homes, people say that the kitchen is where many gather. Could it be because it is usually warm, accessible, homey, intimate, and has an arrangement of furniture that makes it easy and comfortable to see and connect with others?

Thinking about the comfort level of guests helps to guide the floor plan and arrangement of furnishings that creates a physical space in the classroom. If guests are disgusted by a mess, feel uncomfortable in the setting, are too cold or too hot, can't really see what is going on or are blinded by bright lights or loud music, there is little you can do to help the gathering go smoothly. Safety and comfort are basic needs for learning and when the effort to create a comfortable, safe, clean, inviting, well decorated, warm, colorful and interactive space is attended to, the payoff is worth it (Hannah, 2013).

Children are social beings and have similar needs as adults. Sharing and communication can take place when the classroom is set up to encourage and promote connections; therefore, it is important for children to be able to see each other (Hurst, Wallace, & Nixon, 2013). The latest brain research on learning supports the impact of eye contact between learners as it is "a powerful visual cue for building social links between communicating partners" (Jiang, Borowiak, Tudge, Otto, & von Kriegstein, 2017, p. 319).

The teacher's willingness to perfect the skill of making a soft, interested, kind, and curious way of looking at students will give the children a safe sense of security that their thoughts are of value in the classroom (Jiang et al., 2017). Setting a circle of desks, chairs or even mats allows conversation to flow and ideas to be generated. Having a quiet area of comfortable pillows, soft chairs or couches will give children permission to experience a moment of quiet refection, have a much-needed break or find an easy place to just calm down (Adelman & Taylor, 2015).

The attitude and intention of the teacher is pivotal when preparing the delivery for teaching from a social justice perspective (Harmon, 2015). Consider that the educator is a mentor to support interpersonal relationships between teacher and child and between student and student (Blake, 2015). Appropriate dress is powerful; thus, a teacher must dress in an approachable manner, yet maintain a sense of professionalism and authority. Children will respect the educator's personal presentation as an acknowledgement that he or she truly cares about them and their success. The teacher's first impression in the morning can make an impact and change attitudes towards excitement, enthusiasm, optimism, engagement and willingness to learn (Hannah, 2013). When the students make eye contact with the teacher and they resonate with a positive and accepting stance, their anticipation for a successful experience is reinforced without saying a word (Jiang et al., 2017).

Classroom Climate is Critical for Learning

Respect comes in all sizes and when children know that the teacher cares, then they will do the same. The teacher's leadership can take on the roles of fostering academic intelligence as well as emotional and social intelligence. As the leader, the teacher puts forth a visible and understood value for everyone in the class (Bambaeeroo & Shokpour, 2017). Vigilance to that sense of value can sometimes be tricky and, in some instances, messy. Everyone must be valued unconditionally.

The respect, acceptance, recognition, approval, and willingness to learn from mistakes, creates a climate based on safety (Hannah, 2013). It is the safety in the classroom that allows children to flourish and thrive in learning. The relationship cultivated by the teacher sets the stage for student involvement, satisfaction, cohesiveness, innovation, and achievement (Barr, 2016). Personalizing priorities such as listening to students with a non-judgmental heart, respecting student suggestions and thoughts, expressing interest in student ideas, encouraging participation, offering help, making connections, creating harmony and demonstrating mutual trust sets the stage for success (Hurst et al., 2013). By holding the above priorities in high esteem, the safety of the classroom is exemplified and reinforced to initiate higher level learning.

When a bond is initiated by the teacher to build positive rapport with students, the students will follow suit and engage in conversations with each other with respect and enthusiasm (Hurst et al., 2013). It is then that the classroom of connection and action comes to life. Working together becomes the theme of a better way to teach from a vantage point of social justice.

Teacher and Student Perceptions of Classroom Climate

Perception impacts our motivation, satisfaction, and achievement. Perception is personal, individual, and fluid. The teacher must keep in mind the fundamental components of a positive, warm, inviting, accepting learning climate and at the same time be aware of the balance of trial and error it might take to create a growth mindset in the classroom (Young, 2014).

Perceptions are based on personal experience; therefore, teachers can be faced with perceptions that might be negative and toxic versus positive and supportive. The initial and continued call for positive regard, empathy, a sense and display of safety, and the need for an emotionally effective environment, gives the teacher a running start towards the benefits of applying social justice to the classroom experience (Young, 2014).

A perception of trust, cooperation, openness, and respect must exist between students, staff, administrators, parents, and community. The power of a classroom climate that supports children on an intellectual continuum as well as a social and emotional intellectual framework, not only changes the classroom, but supports the containment and redirection of disruptive behaviors (Barr, 2016).

In order to ensure that the classroom climate is perceived in a positive and supportive way, the lines of communication and the vigilance of social and emotional intelligence needs to be front and center (Bambaeeroo & Shokpour, 2017). A teacher's empathic skills play an important role in aligning with children and their reactions, interactions, cooperation, communications and synergy together. When the teacher's perceptions support a welcoming, caring and hopeful place, children will notice the acceptance and relax into the care and safety of the classroom (Bambaeeroo & Shokpour, 2017).

Supporting student goals, participation, achievements and relational needs, creates a positive perception for a well-committed learning environment (Hannah, 2013). By creating a safe and encouraging classroom climate, teachers are training students to build interpersonal skills in order to understand and influence the foundations of social justice (Bambaeeroo & Shokpour, 2017).

How Teaching Through the Lens of Social justice can Influence Classroom Climate

Teachers bring a suitcase filled with personal and historical opinions, perceptions, and varied experiences that may or may not support social justice fundamentals (Lee, 2011). When empathy is part of their skill base, teaching from a social justice framework will flow smoothly (Segal & Wagaman, 2017). Preparing educators in such a way will ensure a future of equality and equity for all.

Past educational training has left many with an inequitable experience of social justice (Lee, 2011). The assumptions teachers make from their own personal experience can influence the way they learn and teach social justice (Baldwin, Buchanan, & Rudisill, 2007). After a teacher has investigated his or her own presumptions, beliefs, prejudices, and expectations, there comes a point where balance, harmony and commitment rise to the forefront (Lee, 2011).

It takes courage, determination, perseverance and fearlessness to examine personal beliefs. Asking questions of inquiry such as "What are my views?," What are my intentions?," "What am I truly aware of?," "What is my ability to be curious, flexible, compassionate and accepting?," "Who am I and what do I want to represent in the classroom, in the school and in the world?" will provide the teacher with invaluable information in order to design a curriculum based on social justice (Lee, 2011).

McIntosh (1990), an associate director of the Wellesley College Center for Research on Women, offered a powerful and vivid picture to help foster self-awareness. The list of living experiences from the standpoint of white privilege, while more than 25 years old, is sobering and many are still true to this day (McIntosh, 1990). The list includes

- *I can be pretty sure that if I ask to talk to the "person in charge," I will be facing a person of my race.*
- *I can, if I wish, arrange to be in the company of people of my race most of the time.*
- *I can speak in public to a powerful male group without putting my race on trial.*
- *I can be sure that if I need legal or medical help, my race will not work against me.*
  (McIntosh, 1990, p. 1)

In addition, this version of the article provides direction to people of her race (white), suggesting small but significant ways to honor the core of what teaching social justice aims to present in education (McIntosh, 1990).

1. *ADMIT IT: "The first step is admitting you have a race."*
2. *LISTEN: "I've found that really listening to people of color and believing their experience is eye -opening."*

3. EDUCATE YOURSELF: "Seriously. Read a book and get on the net."
4. BROADEN YOUR EXPERIENCE: "Caution: Please don't do this until you've successfully completed steps 1-3."
5. TAKE ACTION: "Now where do I put my foot after I've taken it out of my mouth?"

(McIntosh, 1990, p. 3)

Classroom Culture is Decisive for Learning

Similar to classroom climate, the classroom culture requires a place at the table of educational design as "pupil culture is a key element in understanding what a class is" (Michelet, as cited in Nora, 2012, n.p.). Until pupil culture is validated, acknowledged, guided, and sometimes re-directed by a sensitive and intuitive teacher, progress is lost, and more time must be devoted to supporting a positive classroom culture (Hannah, 2013).

Classroom culture goes beyond the components of classroom climate and begins to touch on the building blocks that reinforce the foundation for a community made up of individuals who have agreed upon ethical, moral and value-oriented standards (Teaching Tolerance, 2016). At that point, there is an alignment that takes place in order to foster a direction towards a social justice focus (Blake, 2015).

Cultivating trust, respect, equality, and unconditional acceptance becomes the infrastructure towards a positive classroom culture. Students' individual histories, stories, and experiences are validated and have space and time to be shared and discussed (Krasnoff, 2016). When there is a social and emotional safety net throughout the classroom process, students and teachers have a sense of acceptance and will risk sharing their ideas (Scarf, 2016). Students and teachers trust they are held in high esteem regardless of the judgments that might be generated. With that sense of acceptance, students are more willing to challenge themselves and each other to engage in higher-level thinking and problem solving (Krasnoff, 2016).

Classroom contracts can be designed by the group of students and teachers invested in creating a solid atmosphere of acceptance, equity, equality and respect (Guido, 2017). Social justice weaves the tapestry for students to challenge ideas and debate those thoughts rather than take comments personally (Harmon, 2015). Students are committed to providing the opportunity for meaningful participation and in-depth dialogue as well as fostering personal affirmative assessments and genuine and confident attitudes towards others (Blake, 2015; Krasnoff, 2016).

In an unambiguous classroom culture, reflective listening skills and communication skills are validated and practiced with coaching and encouragement (Krasnoff, 2016). The teacher plays an initial role in modeling and fostering positive coaching encounters with students and then supports students doing the same with each other (Guido, 2017). Consider the design of peer editing where students help each other create a better writing piece. Peer coaching directs students to create more positive interactions between members of the class. Using a technique called "FeedForward" is a "fun and effective way to quickly get a lot of ideas around a challenge you're facing" (Goldsmith, n.d.).

Reinforcement and guidance help students clarify their thinking until the messages are received and dealt with in a fair and equitable manner. As students come to understand, trust and truly believe that what they have to say is important, and various diversities are accepted without judgment, a sense of belonging is reinforced for all (Krasnoff, 2016). Working towards a positive culture helps the classroom becomes a community, a family, a tribe, a group of students and teachers who are committed to taking care of each other (Harmon, 2015). The class has already agreed to engage in similar values and morals with a solid base of ethical standards and as a community, they have an identity and want to succeed and support the culture of connection that sounds something like: we are in this together no matter what.

Consider the value of establishing inclusion, developing a positive mindset, supporting a positive attitude, enhancing personal experience, and engendering competence as the ingredients necessary for a working classroom culture that is headed towards success for everyone (Ginsberg & Wlodkowski, 2015; Ginsberg & Wlodkowski, 2000). In so doing there would be time and energy spent in getting to know each other in the classroom through ice breaker activities, shared biographies or even personal photos of younger times (Scarf, 2016). A class that agrees to work towards greater achievement and excellence fuels motivation, engagement, and excellence for all members of the group (Young, 2014).

Creativity is sparked and flamed by individual and personal meaning. Emotional connection and validation underscore the intention to practice life in the educational experience from a social justice framework (Young, 2014). The entire class senses a solid feeling of contributing to the greater good of the whole. Students and teachers tap into strengths, interests, skills of everyone involved in order to validate and support the culture and the mission of learning (Hurst et al., 2013).

Building a Classroom of Community that Supports Social Justice

When considering the investment in time and energy it takes to create a positive classroom culture, teachers might be tempted to leave it to chance; yet, it must be orchestrated by an intuitive, knowledgeable and empathic teacher (Tomlinson & Murphy, 2018). Guiding the class to explore social justice issues requires a living, breathing expression of what this concept looks like in the day-to-day workings of the classroom.

Classroom culture and classroom climate are influenced and shaped by more than just the students and teachers in the room. The surroundings of the school community itself plays a fundamental role in supporting or challenging what takes place in educational experiences (Dell'Angelo, 2014). The influences, and sometimes direction, are often embedded in administrative priorities, political favor, social impact, cultural diversity, economic struggles and religious values (Tomlinson & Murphy, 2018).

Results of a study by Bickel, Smith and Eagle (2002) looked at the impact of poverty in relationship to the support given to residents in a local community. With support and integrative relationships in neighborhoods, along with positive connections, friendly, informal and socially useful interactions, children make significant achievements in school. Conversely, when neighborhoods and communities defer from a model of connection and respect, achievement in school diminishes (Bickel et al., 2002). For change to take place, stakeholders, community leaders and funding must begin to address and support the children and youth in the neighborhoods, so that students' experiences outside school will enhance the teaching and learning that goes on inside the school.

In order to make learning a priority, an atmosphere must exist where children are ready to master skills and acquire knowledge. When children are engaged and ready for new ideas and challenges, then offering a framework based on social justice can influence thinking and foster a new wave of decision makers (Watanabe-Crockett, 2017). This happens when a community of learners come together as "research in learning theory, cognitive sciences, collaborative learning, and engagement all agree that people learn best in community" (Meredith, 2013).

Consider some of the characteristics of community that have been documented through the literature over time. A sense of belonging plays a major role in feeling connected, safe and seen by the group (Meredith, 2013). By fostering a sense of belonging, children can relax the hyper vigilance of uncertainty, become part of the community and feel confident in their acceptance as a member of the community (Meredith, 2013). When students know that they matter to the members of the group, they are more willing to risk sharing personal opinions, reflections and stories from experience (Tomlinson & Murphy, 2018).

Teaching children to help each other, be patient and interested in members of the community and reach out to assist someone in need as well as have the courage to ask for help, sends a message of safety and respect (Jankovic, 2016). Encouragement and recognition of each other becomes part of the norm and is a skill that can be acknowledged and practiced with compassion and intention (Brady, Forton, & Porter, 2015). The social, emotional and academic sense of the community is reinforcing, supportive, positive, respectful, encouraging and promising towards a solid base for learning about social justice (Brady et al., 2015; Dell'Angelo, 2014).

Community building can take many forms regardless of the classroom setup. Students who collaborate on projects, research a problem-solving solution together, connect on an emotional and social exchange for awareness, test hypotheses in groups, share life stories, investigate a challenging idea all are building community by working together to find solutions (Fryedal & Chiriac, 2017; Sparks, 2017). No matter where the learning is headed - doing it together - supports learning and higher-level thinking. People learn best when they feel part of a community where everyone feels accepted and individually encouraged.

> *Strong communities have members who have shared goals and experiences, who feel empowered to contribute, who trust in one another, and who feel understood and capable as individuals. These attributes enable teamwork, cooperation, a willingness to negotiate, and the ability to draw on one another's skills* (Kane, 2016, n.p.).

Kane's (2016) observations of a learning community led to the foundation of a strong social justice stage for the classroom to engage students; thus, asking the following questions leads to a new awareness of student learning and classroom culture.

- *How can we build a learning atmosphere where all students and teaching team members feel respected and connected to one another (establish inclusion)?*
- *How can we develop a favorable disposition toward the learning experience through personal relevance and choice (develop positive attitudes)?*
- *How can we create challenging, thoughtful learning experiences that include learners' perspectives and values (enhance personal meaning)?*

- *How can we create or affirm an understanding that students have effectively learned something they value and perceive as authentic (engender confidence)?*
(Schmidt, 2018, n.p.)

Building a culture of community in the classroom is such a big issue. Educators must first consider what a classroom built on social justice will look and feel like for themselves and their students (Schmidt, 2018).

Why Social Justice Focus Can Impact Long-Term Change

It stands to reason that offering students the opportunity to explore personal, interpersonal, community, and collective experiences in a supportive learning environment, results in change taking place. A 2016 study by Harrell-Levy, Kerpelman, & Henry found solid evidence that the long-term impact of a transformative social justice course had a significant effect on a group of socioeconomic diverse black adolescents. Well into adulthood the students who had been followed and then interviewed reflected that the social justice course had a significant influence on their decisions after graduation (Harrell-Levy et al., 2016). The study revealed "a deep-rooted link between the course, career choices, and the former students' civic and social-justice values" (Harrell-Levy et al., 2016, p. 99). The takeaway from the study was clear, students have emotions and energy that they have yet to harness and it is up to the adults to "give them the tools...to process in ways that are healthy and will actually build our democracy" (Harrell-Levy et al., 2016, p. 113).

By teaching from a social justice framework, educators will prepare youth with the

- intellectual skills for finding solutions to major challenges,
- the interpersonal skills of listening and communicating in order to hear what others are saying,
- the social skills to negotiate sensitive and meaningful interactions with people and with groups,
- the skills of confident self-esteem so that they will have the courage to give voice to their thinking and the imperative skills of fair values, ethics and morals, which will bring wisdom and compassion to the world.
(Harrell-Levy et al., 2016)

A social justice classroom operates in such a way as to have children practice, integrate, evaluate, and explore what it truly means to respect diversity (Harrell-Levy et al., 2016). Students who are part of a social justice experience, live on to think about, judge, choose, and act according to a moral compass that holds all individuals in an equal and equitable position; thus, this focus will certainly impact long-term change.

Social Justice Practices to Support the Classroom Climate

A teacher must know what is to be taught; yet, "a cultural perspective is almost non-existent in the knowledge base for teacher training. And the little that does exist concentrates on the pupil-teacher relationship" (Michelet as cited in Nora, 2012, n.p.). Teachers are not necessarily prepared to offer an environment that supports a positive classroom culture, let alone a social justice perspective (Nora, 2012).

A significant part of teacher training is preparing the teacher in the art of teaching, not the art of building relationships, inspiring community, designing opportunities for creativity, encouraging decision-making, designing problem-solving activities, fostering effective communication, and using social justice as a foundation for the classroom (Goodman, 2015). Teaching might look like offering the students information from the outside and hoping they will absorb the knowledge and be able to bring it back for the test; however, if the teacher is talking, children are not necessarily learning. To consider that learning happens from the inside out would turn the educational system into a tailspin (Canfield, n.d.).

What do Teachers Need to Provide a Well-Rounded Social Justice Oriented Classroom

There are a variety of standards and pillars for social justice across the globe. Da Cruz (2017) suggests that teachers in an English language arts classroom focus on activities that empower students to communicate with other nations to include the six pillars of (1) health and welfare, (2) democracy and human rights, (3) literacy, (4) equality, (5) creativity, and (6) sustainability. With a laser focus on the development of "the cultural literacy of other nations and the ability to communicate and cooperate with individuals from other nationalities" students will innately develop a social justice mindset" (Da Cruz, 2017, p. 4).

For a more down-to-earth elementary perspective, a third grader might better understand these seven pillars:

1 - *Live in solidarity (treat everyone as your family).*
2 - *Hear the truth (don't just hear what you want to hear).*
3 - *Make injustice visible (bear witness, teach, remember speak it out).*
4 - *Protect the poor and the powerless (listen, learn and empower).*
5 - *Work for reconciliation (apologize with the truth, compassion, understanding and mercy).*
6 - *Celebrate and protect all life (all life is sacred, and we can't end any kind of it).*
7 - *Ensure fair distributions of food and opportunity.*
(Quizlet, 2018, n.p.)

Corning (2011), on the other hand, proposed a three-pronged approach based on "biologically-grounded fairness principles" (n.p.) to include equity, equality, and reciprocity. Maintaining a balance between those three in some sort of social contract naturally equates to a social justice concept that is "fair to everyone" (Corning, 2011, n.p.). Fairness, it appears, is an "evolved and distinctly human behavioral trait" (Corning, 2011, n.p.) that must maintain balance in order to thrive or else it topples over.

Yet, understanding what teachers need in order to provide a social justice-oriented classroom still looms large. Considering that the expectation for social justice is that "everyone deserves equal economic, political and social rights and opportunities" (Gonzalez, 2016, n.p.) it is important to visualize what that looks like. Gonzalez (2016), therefore, offers teachers a thumbnail sketch of what is important in the classroom.

- Get to know the students: It is vital to understand personal backgrounds, biases, and beliefs as well as the students' past experiences. Knowing the students gives the teacher a clearer lens to view the world of each and every student. Many times, their world view is far from the teacher's. Each student has his or her own viewpoint on issues: By having an attitude of unconditional acceptance and positive regard, teachers will be prepared for the wide variety of opinions, as well as the wealth of knowledge the children will bring to the table.
- Know the material you will be teaching. Regardless of what the curriculum and lesson plan is asking for, make sure comprehensive preparation is complete. When the teacher is aware of the lesson, there is the ability to be free to support issues that might arise around social justice.

- Communicate with the administrator: When developing a curriculum that includes social justice awareness, consider turning lessons into group projects that will support the design of community. Informing administration helps validate the desire to be truthful, proactive, transparent, impactful and valid, especially with sensitive lessons. (Gonzalez, 2016)

Teaching from a Social Justice Perspective Will Send Learners into the World to Initiate Positive and Lasting Change

One hundred years ago, William James, the father of psychology said, "The education of attention would be an education par excellence" (as cited in Ratzlaff, n.d.). Attention is the word of the day and helping students to 'pay attention' to what truly matters to them, to their lives, to their families, to their friends, in their classrooms, in their learning impacts education, the teaching, the students, the schools, the community and the world (Bringus, 2016). Our brain is constantly growing, changing and re-wiring. We now have scientific evidence that we can use the mind to change the brain to change the mind forever (Cozolino, 2013).

Teachers are requesting support in their commitment to the children in their charge. Knowing more about the latest research on the brain and on learning will help give a classroom based on social justice strong underpinnings for success. Consider the attention that social and emotional learning (SEL) has been given throughout our educational pedagogy. In a social justice classroom, children and adults depend upon effective ways to manage emotions, negotiate knowledge, temper attitudes and incorporate skills needed to build positive relationships with others.

Having a strong emotional and social framework for all aspects of the educational system, such as the classroom, the teachers, administrators, parents, and community promotes students' social, emotional and academic well-being (CASEL, 2018). There are five competency clusters that are seen as the core competencies of SEL to include social awareness, self-awareness, self-management, relationship skills, and responsible decision making (CASEL, 2018). Developing students' social and emotional competencies helps schools create safe learning environments that contribute to academic achievement for all.

When a classroom is oriented to a social justice framework, and the priority of the learning environment is one of acceptance, safety and connection, children will gracefully and graciously have more brain power for learning. Knowing about the brain and the latest research is not just another thing to add to the teacher's every growing to-do pile. Small chunks of information can be invaluable.

Cozolino (2013) offers nine things educators need to know about the brain.

- *The brain is a social organ.*
- *We have two brains.*
- *Early learning is powerful.*
- *Conscious awareness and unconscious processing occur at different speeds, often simultaneously.*
- *The mind, brain and body are interwoven.*
- *The brain has a short attention span and needs repetition and multiple channel processing for deeper learning to occur.*
- *Fear and stress impair learning.*
- *We analyze others but not ourselves: the primacy of projection.*
- *Learning is enhanced by emphasizing the big picture—and then allowing students to discover the details for themselves* (n.p.).

This suggests that basic neuroscience and brain research supports a social justice classroom as neuroscientists have been helping educators grasp the significance of building neurological connections in the brain by active learning in the classroom (Cozolino, 2013).

The practice of mindfulness has been found to decrease stress and anxiety, increase attention, improve interpersonal relationships, strengthen compassion and help children and adults navigate the landscape of their emotions. The findings from Mindful Schools (2018) includes:

- *Attention: Numerous studies show improved attention, including better performance on objective tasks that measure attention.*
- *Compassion: People randomly assigned to mindfulness training are more likely to help someone in need and have a greater sense of self compassion.*
- *Emotion Regulation: Mindfulness is associated with emotion regulation across a number of studies. Mindfulness creates changes in the brain that correspond to less reactivity, and better ability to engage in tasks even when emotions are activated.*

- *Calming: Studies find that mindfulness reduces feelings of stress and improves anxiety and distress when placed in a stressful social situation.*
(n.p.)

Final Thoughts

In order to support a well informed and academically designed working classroom based on social justice, the teacher must understand classroom climate and culture. This same teacher, who values a social justice approach, needs some help and guidance in order to be successful. Education is ready and waiting for a new energy to come along that provides a creative and inspiring design plan. The desire to orchestrate social justice-based classrooms with teachers who are energized, optimistic, hopeful, and confident about the future, will ensure that our children of today become the promising leaders of tomorrow.

Points to Remember

- *Designing a classroom climate that sets the stage for a social justice framework must be completed intentionally and with care. It is important to enlist the help from the administration, students, and families.*
- *Classroom climate is created with a positive teacher attitude, a physical space that is conducive to learning, open communication, respectful discourse, and intentional delivery of a social justice and/or SEL framework.*
- *The teacher who creates a positive bond with students will be more successful in sustaining a social justice classroom. This occurs when the teacher prioritizes making connections, offering help, demonstrating mutual trust, respecting student suggestions and thoughts, to name a few.*
- *The teacher must model expected behaviors and give meaningful feedback that students can act on without taking them too personally.*
- *In order to make learning a priority, neighborhoods that experience high poverty must enlist the help of the community to lift up students.*
- *Social justice can offer long-term positive impacts of a transformative nature for students who internalize and take the tenets with them into adulthood.*

References

Adelman, H.S. & Taylor, L. (2015). *Mental health in schools: Engaging learners, preventing problems and improving schools.* New York, NY: Skyhorse Printing

Baldwin, S.C., Buchanan, A.M., & Rudisill, M.E. (2007). What teacher candidates learned about diversity, social justice, and themselves from service-learning experiences. *Journal of Teacher Education, 58*(4), 315-327. DOI: 10.1177/0022487107305259

Bambaeeroo, F. & Shokpour, N. (2017). The impact of teachers' non-verbal communication on success in teaching. *Journal of Advances in Medical Education and Professionalism, 5*(2), 51-59. Retrieved from https://www.ncbi.nlm.nih.gov/pmc/articles/PMC5346168/pdf/JAMP-5-51.pdf

Barr, J.J. (2016). *Developing a positive classroom climate.* Retrieved from https://www.ideaedu.org/Portals/0/Uploads/Documents/IDEA%20Papers/IDEA%20Papers/PaperIDEA_61.pdf

Bickel, R., Smith, C., & Eagle, C. (2002). *Poor, rural neighborhoods and early school achievement.* Retrieved from http://mds.marshall.edu/cgi/viewcontent.cgi?article=1004&context=le_st_faculty

Blake, C. (2015). *Teaching social justice in theory and practice.* Retrieved from https://education.cu-portland.edu/blog/classroom-resources/teaching-social-justice/

Brady, K., Forton, M.B., & Porter, D. (2015). *Teaching discipline in the responsive classroom.* Turners Falls, MA: Center for Responsive Schools.

Bringus, R. (2016). *The effects of mindfulness on students' attention.* Retrieved from https://sophia.stkate.edu/cgi/viewcontent.cgi?article=1189&context=maed

Canfield, J. (n.d.). *5 reasons why self-motivated learners win at life.* Retrieved from http://jackcanfield.com/blog/5-reasons-why-self-motivated-learners-win-at-life/

CASEL. (2018). *Core SEL competencies.* Retrieved from https://casel.org/core-competencies/

Cozolino, L. (2013). *The social neuroscience of education: Optimizing attachment & learning in the classroom.* New York, NY: W.W. Norton & CO.

Da Cruz, Z.J. (2017). *Social justice oriented teaching in the English language classroom: Perspectives and practices.* Retrieved from https://skemman.is/bitstream/1946/28617/1/Deusnocomando-2017.zulaia_final.pdf

Dell'Angelo, T. (2014). *Creating classrooms for social justice.* Retrieved from https://www.edutopia.org/blog/creating-classrooms-for-social-justice-tabitha-dellangelo

Ginsberg, M. B., & Wlodkowski, R. J. (2015). Motivation and culture: In *The Sage Encyclopedia of Intercultural Competence,* (pp. 634–637). Los Angeles, CA: Sage.

Ginsberg, M. B., & Wlodkowski, R. J. (2000). Creating highly motivating classrooms for all students: A schoolwide approach to powerful teaching with diverse learners. *The Jossey-Bass Education Series. ERIC.*

Goldsmith, M. (n.d.). *FeedForward.* Retrieved from http://www.marshallgoldsmithfeedforward.com/html/Coaching-for-Behavioral-Change.html

Gonzalez, J. (2016). *A collection of resources for teaching social justice.* Retrieved from https://www.cultofpedagogy.com/social-justice-resources/

Goodman, S. (2015). *The importance of teaching through relationships.* Retrieved from https://www.edutopia.org/blog/importance-teaching-through-relationships-stacey-goodman

Guido, M. (2017). *15 culturally-responsive teaching strategies and examples + downloadable list.* Retrieved from https://www.prodigygame.com/blog/culturally-responsive-teaching/

Hannah, R. (2013). *The effect of classroom environment on student learning.* Retrieved from https://scholarworks.wmich.edu/cgi/viewcontent.cgi?article=3380&context=honors_theses

Harmon, J. (2015). *Social justice: A whole school approach.* Retrieved by https://www.edutopia.org/blog/social-justice-whole-school-approach-jeanine-harmon

Harrell-Levy, M.K., Kerpelmam, J.L., & Henry, D. (2016). 'Minds were forced wide open': Black adolescents' identity exploration in a transformative social justice class. *Education, Citizenship and Social Justice, 11*(2) 99-113. DOI: 10.1177/1746197915626075

HeartMath. (n.d.) *The science of heartmath.* Retrieved from https://www.heartmath.com/science/

Hurst, B., Wallace, R., & Nixon, S.B. (2013). The impact of social interaction on student learning. *Reading Horizons, 52*(4), 375-398. Retrieved from https://scholarworks.wmich.edu/cgi/viewcontent.cgi?referer=https://www.google.com/&httpsredir=1&article=3105&context=reading_horizons

Jiang, J., Borowiak, K., Tudge, L., Otto, C., & von Kriegstein, K. (2017). Neural mechanisms of eye contact when listening to another person talking. *Social Cognitive and Affective Neuroscience, 12*(2), 319-328. Retrieved from https://www.ncbi.nlm.nih.gov/pmc/articles/PMC5390711/pdf/nsw127.pdf

Kane, K. (2016, August 12). *Back to school: Why creating classroom community is so important.* Retrieved from: https://www.naeyc.org/resources/blog/why-creating-classroom-community-so-important

Krasnoff, B. (2016). *Culturally responsive teaching: A guide to evidence-based practices for teaching all students equitably.* Retrieved from https://educationnorthwest.org/sites/default/files/resources/culturally-responsive-teaching.pdf

Lee, Y.A. (2011). What does teaching for social justice mean to teacher candidates? *The Professional Educator, 35*(2). Retrieved from https://files.eric.ed.gov/fulltext/EJ988204.pdf

McIntocsh, P. (1990). *White privilege: Unpacking the invisible knapsack.* Retrieved from https://admin.artsci.washington.edu/sites/adming/files/unpacking-invisible-knapsack.pdf

Meredith, J.R. (2013). *The impact of podcasting on perceived learning, classroom community, and preferred context for podcast consumption.* Retrieved from https://www.missouristate.edu/fctl/193962.htm

Mindful Schools. (2018). *Research on mindfulness.* Retrieved from https://www.mindfulschools.org/about-mindfulness/research/

Nora, S. (2012). *Classroom culture decisive for learning.* Retrieved from http://sciencenordic.com/classroom-culture-decisive-learning

Quizlet. (2018). 7 pillars of social justice. Retrieved from https://quizlet.com/123506687/7-pillars-of-social-justice-flash-cards/

Ratzlaff, G.L. (n.d.). *Contemplative neuroscience.* Retrieved from http://www.ps.ritsumei.ac.jp/assoc/policy_science/194/194_06_ratzlaff.pdf

Scarf, A. (2016). Critical practices for anti-bias education. Retrieved from https://www.tolerance.org/sites/default/files/2017-07/PDA%20Critical%20Practices_0%281%29_0.pdf

Schmidt, S.J. (2018). Creating a classroom culture built on community. *Journal of Food Science education, 17*(1). DOI: 10.1111.1541-4329.12133

Segal, E.A. & Wagaman, M.A. (2017). Social empathy as a framework for teaching social justice. *Journal of social work education, 53*(2), 201-211. DOI: 10.1080/10437797.2016.1266980

Sparks, S.D. (2017). Children must be taught to collaborate, studies say. *Education Week.* Retrieved from https://www.edweek.org/ew/articles/2017/05/17/children-must-be-taught-to-collaborate-studies.html

Teaching Tolerance. (2016). *Critical practices for anti-bias education.* Retrieved from https://www.tolerance.org/sites/default/files/2017-06/PDA%20Critical%20Practices_0.pdf

Watanabe-Crockett, L. (2017). *These 6 practices will make you a more empathic teacher.* Retrieved from https://globaldigitalcitizen.org/6-practices-empathetic-teacher

Chapter Three
Academic and Social Success Cycles: Promoting Socially Just Classroom Experiences for ALL Students

Jacqueline Hawkins, *University of Houston*

Sara J. Jones, *University of Houston*

Kristi L. Santi, *University of Houston*

Schoolhouses are complex systems that are increasingly tasked not only with academic support for students but also social/emotional support and the provision of more wraparound services. Complex systems require leaders with the foresight to engage in strategies and structures that can integrate the various demands that are made of schools. These leadership structures must be complex if they are to ensure that ALL students have opportunities for long-term success in both academic and social/emotional contexts. That is especially true when achievement gaps exist and continue to grow across lines of advantage. Achievement gaps highlight poor educational outcomes for students and are generally associated with poor earning potential, fewer higher education and career choices, lifelong struggles, and repeated cycles of poverty (Crawford, Gregg, MacMillan, Vignoles, & Wyness, 2016; Cheng, Johnson, & Goodman, 2016). School administrators and leaders often must look beyond the walls of the schoolhouse to get to the root cause of the achievement gap that challenges public education systems (Rivera, 2015). Getting to the root cause can involve both pre-work and systems change activities.

Pre-Work

Pre-work is the work that all school personnel must undertake before they are able to engage with students in a positive and meaningful manner. Without this work, educators run the risk of inadvertently harming students (with good intentions) based on faulty logic and hidden biases. In 1993, Tony Wagner wrote about systemic change and how educators could rethink the purpose of school. The authors' focus on pre-work reflects Wagner's (1993) original work and extends it to include specific steps in which educators might engage to realize that change. Three levels of acceptance are outlined that educators should grapple with in order to approach students with a spirit of social justice (J. Hawkins, personal communication, n.d.). Irrespective of racial, ethnic, linguistic, or academic diversity in schools, pre-work can help educators to meet students where they are.

The first level of acceptance requires educators to take a social justice approach; thus, they must accept the changing purpose of school (J. Hawkins, personal communication, n.d.). Currently, schools are both educational and social institutions. The students who attend are not only learning academics but also are learning socialization skills. For many decades, the focus of school had been academic preparation only (Franković, 1970). Consequently, educators were trained to focus on the 3Rs and many have been challenged with the shift towards support for the whole child. More recent school reform efforts have focused on the individualization of support for educator professional development (DuFour, DuFour, Eaker, Many, & Mattos, 2016).

Changes in the delivery of professional development may not be sufficient. Shifting the mindsets of the adults in the system to focus on both academics and socialization also is essential (Dweck, 2016). Solid academic preparation is necessary for academic success; yet, it is often insufficient. Likewise, attention to psychological factors that impact social success is necessary, yet, it is often lacking. Educational systems that consistently encourage and support educators to shift their attention to both academic and social success will likely generate better outcomes for students (Yeager & Dweck, 2012). Building the initial acceptance of this dual-purpose educational system – both academics and socialization – can lead educators to understand the diverse needs of today's student body and the moral imperative that they hold in promoting social justice in each and every schoolhouse.

The second level of acceptance is to remember that students are mandated to be in school every day throughout the school year (J. Hawkins, personal communication, n.d.; Encyclopedia of Children and Childhood in History and Society, 2002). School is where they learn; school is also where they learn to socialize. Oftentimes students, especially students who are members of at-risk or economically-disadvantaged student groups, do not have the freedom to move around from one school to another school if things are not working out as they might like; their way of '*moving around*' may be to pay less and less attention to academic work or *act out* socially. Alternatively, adults in the system have greater freedom to move around from one location to another and often move or leave the profession to improve their job circumstances. Outcomes for the students may improve – both academically and socially - if adults understand this imbalance of freedom to choose and its impact; if adults take the perspective that they hold the responsibility to change; and, if adults create a positive school context that supports the students who are mandated to be there.

The first moral imperative should be that the adults must focus on improving the context of schools for ALL students. Educators must find ways to support students both academically and socially. This focus, or perhaps this change in attitude, understanding, or perspective, likely will help schools to provide students with a sense of belonging, a sense of security, and a sense of safety. Under these circumstances, it's more likely that academic and social success will be achieved. When schools emerge as a community of supportive adults who are focused on these same goals, academic and social success for students can be achieved and the concomitant social justice can be realized.

The third level of acceptance is to embrace differences as strengths (J. Hawkins, personal communication, n.d.). Schools are filled with different people, different capacities, different power differentials, different backgrounds, different experiences, and different goals. Successful leaders in these complex systems create both structures and reform efforts that engage these differences as strengths (KidsMatter, 2012). They help focus the efforts of the entire community on academic and social success for all students. Then they go on to identify the variety of strengths that a system possesses and marshal those in support of students and educators alike. Not everyone can be strong in all areas, but everyone has strengths that, when properly recognized, support the good of the whole school. Focusing on strengths and celebrating differences can go a long way to changing complex systems and promoting social justice.

Systems Change

Internalizing and implementing these three acceptances often leads to the need for change. Changes may be necessary throughout the entire school system/district, on a school campus, or in a classroom. Multi-level, complex systems change involves processes at various levels of engagement that can have their source in the larger school reform efforts, the psychological processes for understanding different ways of thinking and working, and on the daily routine in every classroom. The following sections focus on four areas that, together, could help effective leaders to change attitudes, improve understanding, and create more socially just classrooms and outcomes. The areas presented include understanding school reform efforts, changes in mindset, the implementation of academic success cycles, and the implementation of social success cycles.

Understanding School Reform Efforts

Various educational reform efforts have been implemented in classrooms, schools, districts, states and nationally (Gamoran, 2001). Some involve changes in policy and often focus on academic reform. For example, nationally, the Common Core State Standards (Common Core State Standards Initiative, 2018) and state-level efforts such as College and Career Readiness Standards in Texas (Texas Education Agency, 2009) focus on policies that encourage academic alignment and a focus on the future.

Others adjust how teachers are provided support and often focus on teacher preparation. These changes in professional development have encouraged educators to expand their capacity. Professional learning communities (PLCs) for teachers, for example, is one promising strategy to promote high levels of student learning (DuFour, DuFour, Eaker, Many, & Mattos, 2016). Educators work together in PLCs, use recurring cycles of inquiry, and focus on their on-going job-embedded learning to achieve better student outcomes (Dufour et al., 2016). When educators are involved in collaborative practices, they can change organizations and can have both a profound impact on teachers and a considerable impact on student achievement (Desimone, Porter, Garet, Yoon, & Birman, 2002; Phillips, 2014; Tate, 2004). Educators who deliver instruction differently and give students a different experience can have the greatest impact on student outcomes (Tate, 2004). PLCs function differently and Kruse, Louis, and Bryk (2009) offer five essential elements of PLCs:

- **Reflective Dialogue** – PLC members talk about situations and challenges; develop a set of shared norms, beliefs, and values that form a basis for action; and, engage in various types of self-critique and schoolwide critique.
- **Deprivatization of Practice** – PLC members share, observe, and discuss their respective teaching methods and philosophies; engage in peer coaching; and, share their practice in public.
- **Collective Focus on Student Learning** – PLC members focus on student learning; assume all students can learn and that

teachers can help them irrespective of other obstacles; and, focus on strong professional community.

- **Collaboration** – Strong PLCs encourage working together to develop shared understanding, materials, policies, activities, assessments; and, develop different approaches to professional development.
- **Shared Norms and Values** – PLCs support educators to affirm common values, words, and actions; focus members on student outcomes; and, prioritize the use of time, space, and capacity to support improved student outcomes.

On the whole, most reform efforts focus on academics; most reform efforts focus on student outcomes. These efforts show that performance gaps can be narrowed in one year – by some teachers, in some locations. One teacher, Jaime Escalante, reached overnight fame in the film *Stand and Deliver* (Labunka et al., 1988) when his students (predominantly low-SES and Latino) aced the AP Calculus exam when compared with their peers (Mathews, 1988). Many large-scale studies, for example, The Intensive Partnerships for Effective Teaching Initiative (Stecher et al., 2018) supported by the Bill and Melinda Gates Foundation, show limited or early impact of wide-ranging reforms and many efforts have been considered failures altogether. Other initiatives show promise and those generally extend beyond academic efforts to include social and psychological factors. Most recently, the focus on social and psychological factors involves attention to mindset instruction.

Changes in Mindset

In 1968 Rosenthal and Jacobson provided evidence that teacher expectations could influence the outcomes of students. Specifically, if teachers thought students in their classroom would be successful, they were more successful than others for whom the teachers did not have an opinion (Rosenthal & Jacobson, 1968). Essentially, teachers expected some students to do well and they did well. This early evidence was termed 'The Pygmalion Effect' or a self-fulfilling prophecy (Solomon, 2014). Helping educators to believe that students can do well is an initial step in improving student outcomes (Dweck, 2016; O'Keefe, Dweck, & Walton, 2018). Essentially, minds that were initially *fixed* "my students cannot do well" can be supported to focus on change and *growth* "my students can do well". Educators also can convince the students in their class to acquire a *growth* mindset.

Early work by Dweck and Leggett (1988) differentiated fixed mindsets from growth mindsets. A fixed mindset refers to the belief that intelligence is a set ability and does not change much over time. Individuals with a tendency to a fixed mindset give up more easily and are unlikely to try harder in the future after they have failed. Alternatively, individuals with a tendency to a growth mindset, or a belief that intelligence can be improved with instruction and practice, are more likely to continue to try and use their energy to strategize a solution.

Twenty-five years later, Yeager and Dweck (2012) analyzed evidence from multiple sources. Their findings support that students with growth mindsets perform better in both academic and social contexts. Specifically, when they are challenged in these contexts, they put forth the effort to succeed, they ask for help, they try new strategies, and they generally have higher levels of resilience in the face of challenges. Supporting students who have a more fixed mindset can be challenging; however, Yeagar and Dweck (2012) offer hope that fixed mindsets can be changed. Indeed, Dweck (2016) asks educators to consider the role that feedback can play in changing mindsets. Dweck (2016) argues that feedback should focus on the specific areas for change – levels of effort, use of new strategies, and help seeking – rather than general feedback. Educators who want students to:

- increase effort might say –
    - *'keep going, you're almost there'* (indirect) or
    - *'you can do two more math problems before you finish'* (direct);
- use new strategies might say –
    - *'what other tools have you learned that might work here?* (indirect) or
    - *'what about using grammar and spell-check before you submit your essay?'* (direct); or,
- seek help might say –
    - *'who might know how to help you with this?* (indirect)
    - *'do you want to ask a peer or the teacher about the next steps in the problem?* (direct).

Each of these examples provides guidance to the student about the specific steps in responding to a challenge, either indirectly or directly, and can be more instructive and supportive than a global comment such as *'good job.'*

Adults, therefore, can foster mindsets in students. Indeed, Haimovitz and Dweck (2016) demonstrate that what adults do is more important than what adults say has a greater impact on mindset. Essentially, supporting a growth mindset goes beyond the feedback that students receive. This is especially important after students have experienced failure. When adults behave in a manner that implies to students that they question a student's competence the student relates to that behavior and, consequently, questions his or her own competence (Haimovitz & Dweck, 2016). Alternatively, when adults behave in a manner that implies that failure is part of learning and gaining competence, the student relates to that behavior and, consequently, accepts failure as part of learning and success (Haimovitz & Dweck, 2016). Educators who create a positive learning environment, assess often and adjust accordingly, provide specific feedback that targets academic and/or social outcomes, and engage learners in their own growth can change the mindsets of their students (Dweck, 2016). Consistent application of targeted cycles of inquiry, for each individual child, can support both academic and social growth and realize the goal of more socially just schools. Schools where students have the mindset that they belong, where they are secure in their learning, and where they are safe with a supportive network of educators. Adapted from an improvement science approach as proposed by Bryk, Gomez, Grunow, and LeMahieu's (2015), the use of academic and social success cycles will generate the improvements that communities require of their schools.

Academic Success Cycles

Successful educators engage in a sequence of steps that ensure academic success for students (Brookhart, 2010). The sequence of steps proposed here is cyclical and can be repeated over time, across students, and across content areas. These phases involve measurement, focusing skills on the immediate goal at hand, implementation, and reflection (Bryk et al., 2015). An academic success cycle helps to determine where students are functioning academically, helps to implement interventions that focus on their strengths, builds a path to success, and allows for differentiation of materials and models that appeal to students. Each of the phases in the cycle is discussed with examples.

Measurement involves the assignment of a number in accordance with a set of rules. Accurate measures can provide us with an understanding of current status and progress over time. Many measures are used to determine academic outcomes. Some are summative and, as such, they provide an overall picture of a student's mastery at the end of a period of time, the end of a unit, etc. This section focuses on less formal measures, formative assessment, that are used by educators in classrooms and schools to guide instruction and interventions towards a target or a goal (Brookhart, 2010).

Educators employ formative assessments to help them to determine the progress that a student is making – too little, just right, more than anticipated; and informs instruction – repeat instruction, provide more time for practice, move on, or change to a more advanced level, etc. Formative assessments engage teachers (and, at times, students) in continuous progress monitoring and provide students with feedback about their progress towards a particular goal. There are many types of formative assessment. Curriculum Based Measurement (CBM) is the most common measure for academic subjects (Deno, 1985).

CBM is used in academic areas (e.g., mathematics, reading, or writing). Educators design a short assessment or use one that is provided in a teacher's manual (or online) that is directly related to the material that students are to learn (Deno, 1985). Alignment of the assessment content and format with the instruction is key, because closer alignment leads to a more accurate understanding of student progress. Students complete the assessment, often writing answers or working problems, and receive immediate feedback once it is scored (Deno, 1985). It is important that educators explain the feedback about performance to students since the outcome on the assessment determines the next steps in the curriculum that the student will learn. If insufficient learning occurred, instruction can be adjusted to ensure student success. The integral interaction between instruction and student progress is key to the success of using CBM.

Focusing on a Goal helps all concerned to understand the path forward. When student progress is slow, it is often appropriate to set short-term goals that can be mastered more frequently to help motivate them to continue to success. Also, when graphed outcomes and goal setting are included in the CBM process, educators and students alike can see the amount of learning that has to occur before the academic content is mastered – the gap between current performance and the goal is visual and can become more 'real' for students. Goal setting and graphing of CBM performance outcomes help students to self-regulate their learning. Specifically, they can see where they are, how much they have to learn to meet the target and can engage in focused conversations with educators about what they believe they need to reach their goal. Supporting students to a level of self-regulation that involves a greater understanding of their own needs is key to greater academic success; for example, they may determine that their performance is better in a quiet area, earlier in the day, when they have studied, when they used a problem-solving strategy, etc. Students can be encouraged to determine the conditions or contexts in which they perform better, the support that they need from others to learn, and can begin to differentiate what is essential to their own success.

Implementation of CBM in Reading can involve the number of words a student reads correctly per minute at a particular reading level – Reading Fluency; CBM in Writing could involve the proportion of written sentences that had appropriate subject-verb agreement, the number of adjectives that appropriately modified nouns, or the accuracy of use of commas or periods; CBM in Mathematics could involve the proportion of math problems in which students showed their work appropriately and solved the problem correctly. The strengths of CBM are in the quick completion, the frequency with which these assessments can be done in a classroom, and (especially when the outcomes are graphed) the ability to show students the changes in their learning immediately.

Reflection is the final phase in the academic success cycle (Howard, 2003). Reflection helps to determine what worked, why, and for whom. Reflection involves attention to all other phases in the cycle. Is the measure appropriate, sensitive to small changes, and matched to what is being taught? Is the goal too much of a stretch, too limited, or just right? Do educators have the capacity, tools, and mindset to implement for all students? Reflections go beyond the scores on a test to include the words people use, the actions people take, and the spirit with which they approach academic tasks. Reflection is key to ensuring that academic success cycles continue over time and adjust to the changing needs of students and educators. Reflection occurs at all levels of the system.

Social Success Cycles

Academic focused efforts alone have failed to achieve equality in schools; yet, research on social and emotional learning (SEL) indicates that focusing on the whole child, not only their academic content knowledge but also their ability to identify and manage emotions within themselves and in interactions with others, may be a path toward social justice for ALL students (Payton, et al., 2008). Similar to academic success cycles, approaching SEL instruction through a reflective cycle of measurement, goal setting, implementation, and reflection can support student success.

Measurement of SEL is relatively new when compared to assessing academic course material. Due to the multiple conceptions of SEL and social skills frameworks in the research literature, the first step for a teacher, school, or district to consider when implementing SEL is to establish a local consensus around key components of SEL for the school

(Barblett & Maloney, 2010; Payton, et al., 2008). The most widely recognized framework was developed by Collaborative for Academic, Social, and Emotional Learning (CASEL, 2003; CASEL, 2018) and identifies 5 competencies that make up SEL: self-awareness, self-management, social awareness, relationship skills, and responsible decision making. As with the definition, there are a variety of tools for measuring SEL in students of all ages. Self-report questionnaires are common (Haggerty, Elgin, & Woolley, 2011), as are observational rating scales completed by the parents and teachers and peers (Denham et al., 2011).

Teacher expectations and implicit bias can affect observational data (Wigelsworth, Humphrey, Kalambouka, & Lendrum, 2010); therefore, having well-constructed rating scales with discrete behaviors is essential in any observation measurement. Social competence can be measured through peer ratings or nominations to evaluate how well-liked a student is among his or her peers and through student responses to social scenario prompts (Ladd 1999; Gifford-Smith & Brownell 2003). While all of these methods have advantages and disadvantages, the key to social change is to employ a measurement that can seamlessly provide data about growth to the teachers and the subject.

Goal Setting is a key component of SEL that should be both directly taught and modeled to students. Teachers can promote social justice by engaging students in the goal-setting process rather than dictating class objectives and goals. Focusing on small achievable goals that increase over time teaches students how to manage their own growth and build their self-efficacy for making good decisions.

Implementation is most likely to be effective when the whole school is working toward the same goal. Previously, social and emotional skills were viewed as skills that would organically develop over time without intervention; however, research has demonstrated that SEL skills not only can be taught, but when explicitly taught, can impact academic and life success (Durlak, Weissberg, Dymnicki, Taylor & Schellinger, 2011; Taylor, Oberle, Durlak, & Weissberg, 2017).

All students have developed skills and strategies to function in their home environments. Teachers and administrators must implement SEL instruction that honors and leverages the strengths that students already have, even if some of the behaviors seem maladaptive for a school setting. Rather than discrediting social and emotional strategies that help students, especially those from economically disadvantaged homes or diverse cultural backgrounds, teachers and administrators need to acknowledge the complex social and emotional abilities that students have developed in order to survive in their homes and neighborhoods.

While these behaviors may not all be adaptive for a school setting, the students' abilities to interact in social environments demonstrate an aptitude for learning SEL skills. Demonstration of SEL skills in other environments shows capacity and will be adaptive in schools.

One way to honor student diversity is to explicitly teach the concept of *code switching*. Originally conceptualized literature around dual-language populations, the term has recently been expanded to switching between cultural settings, even in the absence of a second language (Lin, 2013). *Code switching* refers to the idea that individuals may change their demeanor, word choices, and even some aspects of their personality depending on the language they are using in a given setting (Martin-Jones, 1995; Lin, 2013). School efforts should focus on helping students to 1) understand the concept of *code switching*, 2) distinguish between their own social and cultural environments, and 3) leverage that knowledge to adapt social practices that help them achieve their goals in various social settings.

Reflection is the final phase of any good decision-making cycle (Howard, 2003). Sustainable school reform calls for reflection from all levels of the system. Schools periodically must use a combination of qualitative and quantitative data from administrators, teachers, students, and parents to effectively assess whether or not individual students and the school as a whole are meeting the agreed upon goals and making progress toward a more just schoolhouse.

Final Thoughts

Schools are complex systems that must adapt to the changing demographics and needs of our students. In order to close the achievement gap that has persisted in the schools, teachers, administrators, and districts must adapt to support both academic growth for students and also social/emotional learning needs. This change requires individual and whole school level work to change the mindset and culture around these new broadened goals of the school. When educators take time to critically assess their mindset about diverse students and their ability to learn and the purpose of school, a shift in the dynamics of the school begins to happen. Using a cycle of measurement, goal setting, implementation, and reflection, teachers can monitor and adapt to student progress in needs in both academic and social/emotional domains. When schools change to incorporate a focus that combines these two domains, the achievement gap begins to narrow.

Points to Remember

- *School is not just for academics anymore. Educators must support the whole child through a variety of interventions that address the social, behavioral, health and wellness, as well as educational aspects of each student.*
- *School change is complex and needs to happen both at the individual educator level and at the system level.*
- *Educators should embrace a mindset where all students experience academic and social success.*
- *Academic success cycles promote student success, while social success cycles promote student well-being. Using a sequence of steps to include measurement; a focus on skills that have a direct impact on the immediate goal; implementation; and, reflection, students will build a path to success.*

References

Barblett, L., & Maloney, C. (2010). Complexities of assessing social and emotional competence and wellbeing in young children. Retrieved from https://ro.ecu.edu.au/cgi/viewcontent.cgi?referer=https://www.google.com/&httpsredir=1&article=7243&context=ecuworks

Brookhart, S. M. (2010). *Formative assessment strategies for every classroom: An ASCD action tool, 2nd Edition*. Alexandria, VA: ASCD

Bryk, A. S., Gomez, L. M., Grunow, A., & LeMahieu, P. G. (2015). *Learning to improve: How America's schools can get better at getting better*. Cambridge, MA: Harvard Education Press.

Cheng, T.L., Johnson, S.B., & Goodman, E. (2016. Breaking the intergenerational cycle of disadvantage: The three generation approach. *Pediatrics, 137*(6), e20152467. Retrieved from https://www.ncbi.nlm.nih.gov/pmc/articles/PMC4894258/

Collaborative for Academic, Social, and Emotional Learning [CASEL]. (2018). *Core SEL competencies.* Retrieved from https://casel.org/core-competencies/

Collaborative for Academic, Social, and Emotional Learning [CASEL]. (2003). *Safe and Sound: An educational leader's guide to evidence-based Social and Emotional Learning (SEL) programs.* Retrieved from https://casel.org/safe-and-sound-an-educational-leaders-guide-to-evidence-based-social-and-emotional-learning-sel-programs/

Common Core State Standards Initiative (2018). *About the standards.* Retrieved from http://www.corestandards.org/about

Crawford, C., Gregg, P., MacMillan L., Vignoles, A., & Wyness, G. (2016). Higher education, career opportunities, and intergenerational inequality. *Oxford Review of Economic Policy, 32*(4), 553-575. DOI: 10.1093/oxrep/grw030

Denham, S.A., Bassett, H.H., Thayer, S.K., Mincic, M.S., Sirotkin, Y. S., & Zinsser, K. (2012). Observing preschoolers' social-emotional behavior: Structure, foundations, and prediction of early school success. *The Journal of Genetic Psychology, 173*(3), 246-278. DOI: 10.1080/00221325.2011.597457

Deno, S.L. (1985). Curriculum-based measurement: The emerging alternative. *Exceptional Children, 52*(3), 219-232. DOI: 10.1177/001440298505200303

Desimone, L.M., Porter, A.C., Garet, M.S. Yoon, K.S., & Birman, B.F. (2002). Effects of professional development on teachers' instruction: Results from a three-year longitudinal study. *Educational Evaluation and Policy Analysis. 24*(2), 81-112. DOI: 10.3102/01623737024002081

DuFour, R., DuFour, R., Eaker, R., Many, T.W., & Mattos, M. (2016). *Learning by doing; A handbook for professional learning communities at work.* Bloomington, Indiana Solution Tree Press.

Durlak, J. A., Weissberg, R. P., Dymnicki, A. B., Taylor, R. D., & Schellinger, K. B. (2011). The impact of enhancing students' social and emotional learning: A meta-analysis of school-based universal interventions. *Child Development, 82,* 405–432. DOI:10.1111/j.1467-8624.2010.01564.x

Dweck, C.S. (2016). *Mindset: The new psychology of success* (2nd ed.). York, NY: Random House

Dweck, C.S. & Leggett, E. L. (1988). A social-cognitive approach to motivation and personality. *Psychological Review, 95*(2), 256-273. DOI: 10.1037/0033-295X.95.2.256

Encyclopedia of Children and Childhood in History and Society (2002). *Compulsory School Attendance.* Retrieved from https://www.encyclopedia.com/social-sciences-and-law/education/education-terms-and-concepts/compulsory-school-attendance

Franković, D.P. (1970). The school as a social institution. *Prospects in Education 1*(2), 7-11. DOI: 10.1007/BF02354310

Gamoran, A. (2001). American schooling and educational inequality: A forecast for the 21st century. *Sociology of Education, 74,* 135-153. 10.2307/2673258

Gifford-Smith, M. E., & Brownell, C. A. (2003). Childhood peer relationships: Social acceptance, friendships, and peer networks. *Journal of School Psychology 41*(4): 235- 284. DOI: 10.1016/S0022-4405(03)00048-7

Haggerty, K., Elgin, J., & Woolley, A. (2011). *Social-Emotional learning assessment measures for middle school youth.* Retrieved from https://www.search-institute.org/wp-content/uploads/2017/11/DAP-Raikes-Foundation-Review.pdf

Haimovitz, K., & Dweck, C. S. (2016). Parents' views of failure predict children's fixed and growth intelligence mind-sets. *Psychological Science, 27*(6), 859-869. DOI:10.1177/0956797616639727

Howard, T.C. (2003). Culturally relevant pedagogy: ingredients for critical teacher reflection. *Theory into Practice, 42*(3), 195-202. DOI: 10.1027/s15430421tip4203_5

KidsMatter (2012). Cultural diversity: Suggestions for school staff. Retrieved from https://www.kidsmatter.edu.au/sites/default/files/public/KMP_C1_CDCW_CulturalDiversity_SuggestionsForSchoolStaff.pdf

Kruse, S., Louis, K., & Bryk, A. (2009). Building professional community in schools. 13 Parameters: *A Literacy Leadership Toolkit, Research Resource Book*, pp. 159-163. Canada: Pearson Education

Labunka, I., Law, L., Muska, T. (Producers), & Menendez, R. (Director). (1988). *Stand and Deliver* [Motion Picture]. United States: Warner Bros.

Ladd, G. W. (1999). Peer relationships and social competence during early and middle childhood. *Annual Review of Psychology, 50*(1): 333-35. DOI: 10.1146/annurev.psych.50.1.333

Lin, A. M. Y. (2013). Classroom code-switching: Three decades of research. *Applied Linguistics Review, 4*(1), 195-218. DOI: 10.1515/applirev-2013-0009

Martin-Jones, M. (1995). Code-switching in the classroom: Two decades of research. In L. Milroy & P. Muysken (Eds.), *One Speaker, Two Languages: Cross-Disciplinary Perspectives on Code-Switching* (pp. 90-112). Cambridge: Cambridge University Press.

Mathews, J. (2010, April 4). *Jaime Escalante didn't just stand and deliver: He changed U.S. schools forever.* Washington Post. Retrieved from http://www.washingtonpost.com/wp-dyn/content/article/2010/04/02/AR2010040201518.html

O'Keefe, P.A., Dweck, C., & Walton, G. (2018). Having a growth mindset makes it easier to develop new interests. *Harvard Business Review.* Retrieved from https://hbr.org/2018/09/having-a-growth-mindset-makes-it-easier-to-develop-new-interests

Payton, J., Weisberg, R.P., Durlak, J.A., Dymnicki, A.B., Taylor, R.D., Schellinger, K.B., & Pachna, M. (2008, December). *The Positive Impact of Social and Emotional Learning for Kindergarten to Eighth-Grade Students: Findings from Three Scientific Reviews.* Retrieved from https://www.casel.org/wp-content/uploads/2016/08/PDF-4-the-positive-impact-of-social-and-emotional-learning-for-kindergarten-to-eighth-grade-students-executive-summary.pdf

Phillips, J.K. (2014). *Study of the impact of professional learning communities and student achievement.* ProQuest Dissertations Publishing, 3621758

Rivera, S. (2015). *Solutions to the achievement gap – according to teachers.* Retrieved from https://www.kipp.org/news/noodle-solutions-to-the-achievement-gap-according-to-teachers/

Rosenthal, R., & Jacobson, L. (1968). *Pygmalion in the classroom: Teacher expectation and pupils' intellectual development.* New York: Holt, Rinehart, & Winston.

Solomon, B. (2014). The Pygmalion effect: Communicating high expectations. Retrieved from https://www.edutopia.org/blog/pygmalion-effect-communicating-higher-expectations-ben-solomon

Stecher, B. M., Holtzman, D.J., Garet, M.S., Hamilton, L.S., Engberg, J. & Chambers, J. (2018). *Improving teaching effectiveness: Final report: The intensive partnerships for effective teaching through 2015–2016*, Santa Monica, Calif.: RAND Corporation, RR-2242-BMGF, 2018. Retrieved from https://www.rand.org/content/dam/rand/pubs/research_reports/RR2200/RR2242/RAND_RR2242.pdf

Tate, M.L. (2004). *"Sit & Get" won't grow dendrites: 20 professional learning strategies that engage the adult brain.* Corwin Press. Thousand Oaks, California.

Taylor, R.D., Oberle, E., Durlak, J.A., & Weissberg, R.P. (2017). Promoting positive youth development through school-based social and emotional learning interventions: A meta-analysis of follow-up effects. *Child Development, 88*(4), 1156-1171. DOI: 10.1111/cdev.12864

Texas Education Agency. (2009). *College and career readiness standards.* Retrieved from http://erc.cehd.tamu.edu/sites/erc.cehd.tamu.edu/files/ERC_Documents/3_CCRS.pdf

Wagner, T. (1993). Systemic change: Rethinking the purpose of school. *Educational Leadership, 51*(1), 24-28. Retrieved from http://www.ascd.org/publications/educational-leadership/sept93/vol51/num01/Systemic-Change@-Rethinking-the-Purpose-of-School.aspx

Wigelsworth, M., Humphrey, N., Kalambouka, A., & Lendrum, A. (2010). A review of key issues in the measurement of children's social and emotional skills. *Educational Psychology in Practice, 26*(2), 173–186. DOI: 10.1080/02667361003768526

Yeager, D. S., & Dweck, C, S. (2012). Mindsets that promote resilience: When students believe that personal characteristics can be developed. *Educational Psychologist, 47*(4), 302-314. DOI: 10.1080/00461520.2012.722805

Chapter Four
All Money Matters: Socioeconomic Factors and the Impact on Learning

Dariel T. Henry,
Massasoit Community College and Regis College

Consider this vignette: *A class of first graders was given a coloring book picture by the teacher and asked to color at home with their parents and to bring the coloring book picture back to school the following day. When students returned the assignment the next day, the teacher noticed that one group had used only three colors, another had used many colors, and a third group had used a pencil for sections of the coloring book picture. The teacher asked students in the group who had used only three colors why they had not used more colors. One student responded, "I do not have as many crayons at home. I only have three crayons." The teacher then began to consider the significant differences in the home lives of the students and how those differences may impact the children's development and academic achievement.*

The school had two distinct groups of students as viewed by socioeconomic status (SES), which is measured by household income, parents' education level, and occupation (American Psychological Association, 2018). Of the students in the school, 70% were high SES students, while the remaining 30% were low SES students who were transported to the school through a district-wide inclusion initiative. An analysis of the students' academic performance showed that children in the low socioeconomic group had lower scores compared with students in the high-socioeconomic status group in many areas including writing, storytelling, reading, math, exploration and classroom social behavior. The impacts of social inequality on child development, learning and academic achievement cannot be ignored.

What are Socio-Economic Factors and Why They Matter to Education

Poverty rates are strongly correlated with education levels. According to the US Census Bureau, in 2016 the poverty rate of individuals over 25 without a high school diploma or equivalent was almost one in four (24.8%) (Semega, Fontenot, & Kollar 2017). The poverty rate for individuals over 25 with a high school diploma or equivalent was strikingly lower at 13.3% (Semega et al., 2017). The poverty rate decreased to 9.4% percent for those over the age of 25 with some college, and for those with an earned bachelor's degree, a 50% reduction in the poverty rate to 4.5% (Semega et al., 2017).

Schools that are underfunded by local taxes experience high turnover of teachers and guidance counselors (Bristol, 2014) negatively impacting academic resources. Attending a private high school or meeting with a guidance counselor increases student access to information such as applying to college, and these relationships are essential to students from low socioeconomic status (Belasco, 2013). Emdin (2017) observes that most of the teachers and support staff do not live in the same communities as the students they serve. This ushers in a variety of problems and struggles, including high teacher and staff turnover leaving students without consistency so essential to student academic and personal success (Emdin, 2017).

Measuring child development and learning, parenting styles, home environment, language acquisition, school influence, health, and academic achievement are important benchmarks in a child's growth, development and wellbeing (Zahed Zahedani, Rezaee, Yazdani, Bagheri, & Nabeiei, 2016). Comparing those measurements by socioeconomic status (family/household income, education and occupation) provides critically important insight into the realities that money matters (Zahed Zahedani et al., 2016). The three broad categories of socio-economic status (SES) are the high, middle, and lower classes (Federal Poverty Guidelines, 2018). Children and families in the "lower classes" live close to or below the poverty line, which is approximately $20,700 for a family of three (Federal Poverty Guidelines, 2018). A significant lack of income, for multiple generations, can lead to inter-generational poverty and have deleterious effects on communities (and the families and children of those communities) for decades (Cheng, Johnson, & Goodman, 2016).

Before entering school, learning first occurs at home. Parents are the first teachers to children. Income (as well as time limitations due to employment demands) impacts the resources parents can provide for their children to expand learning (Crosnoe, Purtell, Davis-Kean, Ansari, & Benner, 2016). Toys, boards games, verbal and physical interactions with adults for behavior role modeling, all stimulate brain development. Through verbal interactions with adults, children learn critical language, listening and reading skills such as semantics (the meanings of words and phrases in a particular context); syntax (the arrangement of words and phrases to create well-formed sentences in a language); morphology (the study of the forms of words and root words, prefixes, suffixes, plurals, etc.); and phonology (rules which specify how sounds interact with each other) (Otto, 2017).

Hart and Risley (1995) documented the discovery of a 30-million-word gap in language as a result of the amount of words a child heard prior to starting pre-school. Starting at 18-months, children from high socioeconomic status households developed essential learning skills from more verbal engagement early in their home environment compared to children from low socioeconomic status (Hart & Risley, 1995). The disparity resulted in the low socioeconomic status group struggling with cognitive and language skills once they entered kindergarten and elementary school (Golinkoff, Rowe, Tamis-LeMonda, & Hirsh-Pasek, 2018).

What students learn in school must be reinforced at home in order for the learning to be continued from each grade level to the next. While all students experience a decrease in academic skills during the summer months, students of low–socioeconomic status experience a greater setback, with the most critical decrease occurring in reading (Bowers, Lisa, & Schwarz, 2018). There is a lack of resources in low socioeconomic group households to access or purchase the quantity and quality of reading materials and resources, such as books in print version, eBooks, audiobook accounts, digital devices to store and listen to these forms of content, and transportation to and from public libraries (assuming a public library exists in the community (Rothstein, 2017). It is not uncommon to find community organizations dedicated to trying to bridge the resource gap to provide all students with quality summer learning and reading readiness skills programs (Bowers & Schwarz, 2018).

The Impact of Social Inequality

Socioeconomic status (household income, education level and occupation) have a direct impact on learning (Semega et al., 2017). Comedian Chris Rock once commented about his wealth by observing "Wealth is not about having a lot of money; it's about having a lot of options." (Rock, 1999). Income impacts a variety of factors to include quality of life, choice of neighborhood lived in, the schools children attend, summer activities, health coverage, and parental engagement

(Martens et al., 2014). In 2016, median incomes for all American family households was $75,062; Asian households had the highest median 2016 income ($81,431), followed by non-Hispanic white ($65,041), black ($39,490), and Hispanic ($47,675) (Semega et al., 2017).

In 2016, 12.7% of the U.S. population lived below the federal poverty line (40.6 million people) (Semega et al., 2017). The number of the population living below the poverty line in 2016 varied by race and ethnicity; however, 17.3 million whites, 9.2 million blacks, and 11.1 million Hispanics lived in poverty (Semega et al., 2017).

Poverty in childhood can result in higher rates of physical and mental health difficulties, lower academic achievement as well as diminished cognitive, and executive functioning (Zilberstein, 2016). How is it that some families accumulate generational wealth while others descend into and remain in poverty in our country that claims to be the "land of opportunity?" Shapiro (2004) described how accessibility to decent middle-class education was impacted by family income and wealth. According to Shapiro (2004), wealth was accumulated from great-grandparents and grandparents, who benefited from policies that helped grow the American middle class in the 1960s and 1970s. Each generation climbed the socioeconomic ladder accessing education in the form of private school tuitions, tutors, and academic summer camps for their children and grandchildren (Shapiro, 2004). This was also found in the form of homeownership as Shapiro (2004) interviewed over 200 families and learned about financial resources that aided in taking economic risk by providing down payments for family homes and renovations.

The G.I. Bill, also known as, the Servicemen's Readjustment Act of 1944, provided a range of benefits for returning World War II veterans including tuition payments, low-cost mortgages, low-interest start-up business loans, one year of unemployment compensation, and no pay of income tax on the benefits (Young, Michael, & Jean, 2019). Some military veterans from the 1960s and 1970s who utilized the G.I. Bill for higher education were also able to gain employment at those colleges and universities, resulting in a snowball of benefits for generations (Young et al., 2019).

> *Consider a white male named John, who was born in 1940, and after serving four years in the military, became a GI Bill recipient in 1962. John attended college tuition-free and received his bachelor's degree in 1966 and gained employment at the university he attended as a graduate assistant, which paid his master's degree tuition. By 1990, John was 50 years old with two children in their teens. Over two decades, John was able to rise in*

> his career at the university and his children then had the option of accessing a debt-free education from the same university as a benefit from their father. The example continues as one of John's children, now age 38 and with a family, took the same route as the father. John's grandchildren also have the option of accessing a debt-free higher education from the same university that benefited two previous generations. The results are three generations of debt-free access to higher education from the policies that began from a benefit received in the 1960s.

At the height of the Civil Rights Movement when many black citizens were fighting for equal rights and facing discriminatory practices, the GI Bill, as practiced, was not afforded to Blacks and women in the same way as white men.

> Consider a black male named Jim, who was born in 1940, and received the GI Bill in 1962. Jim attends college during the Civil Rights Movement and becomes active in community protest. As a result, he is arrested twice, and although he graduates from college, he faces barriers of unequal opportunity. With his arrest record, and increased disenfranchisement in the 1970s, Jim is prohibited from competing in the dominant workforce. Jim has children, but with his low income, he and his family struggle financially. Down payments for homes, private school education, and summer academic camps are not affordable for Jim. His children grow older and receive student loans for college and spend a portion of their career salary paying the debt. The grandchildren of the family have not been passed down resources in home equity or education benefits. In this family, three generations have accrued debt, not invested in homeownership, and made minimal gains in social mobility.

Dr. Martin Luther King Jr. delivered a speech at the National Cathedral, Washington, D.C., in 1968 and was asked why black people in America had not increased their socioeconomic status juxtaposed to other races that migrated to America. He responded, "It's alright to tell a man to lift himself by his own bootstraps, but it is a cruel jest to say to a bootless man that he ought to lift himself by his own bootstraps" (Carson, 2001; Carson & Hollaran, 2000).

Employment and Unemployment

Julius W. Wilson (1997), the Malcolm Wiener Professor of Social Policy at Harvard University, studied the deleterious effects of deindustrialization, specifically unemployment, and the transformation of a community to low-socioeconomic status. One critical finding revealed that children were negatively affected by unemployment not only because of loss of household income; rather, from having not learned the positive behaviors of working adult role models, the disappearance of work eliminated networking opportunities, organization, structure, and meeting deadlines that children adapt from the modeled behavior of working parents (Wilson, 1997).

Education and Poverty Levels

There is a powerful connection between education and poverty levels. For example, in 2016, nearly one in four Americans over the age of 25 without a high school diploma lived in poverty (24.8%) (Semega et al., 2017). For those with a high school diploma, the poverty rate declined to 13.3%. Those with some college had a poverty rate of 9.4%, and 4.5% percent for those with a four-year degree (Semega et al., 2017). Quality, high impact schools require funding. The primary source of school funding in most parts of the country is local taxes. Communities with a 24.8% poverty rate are not able to fund schools in the same way that communities with lower poverty rates can (Bristol, 2014).

Education Deserts and a Public Health Crisis

In December 2017, the Chronicle of Higher Education published an article that opened with research uncovering links between education — or lack of it — and health in towns in Missouri and other rural communities across the country (Brown & Fischer, 2017).

> *Here in a corner of Missouri and across America, the lack of a college education has become a public-health crisis...It's not clear whether a college degree leads directly to better health or, if so, how. But the findings are alarming: educational disparities and economic malaise and lack of opportunity are making people ... sick. And maybe even killing them* (Brown & Fischer, 2017, n.p.).

What is clear is that a four-year college degree has a positive impact on health and wellness.

In communities like those featured in this story, only one out of ten adults have earned a four-year college degree (Brown & Fischer, 2017). For those who desire a college education, the journey begins 100 miles away in cities where post-secondary institutions are located. The absence of post-secondary institutions within a reasonable proximity and accessible by public transportation is labeled an "education desert" (Myers, 2018). An interactive map of the United States indicates the location of all post-secondary institutions (Hillman & Weichman, 2016). The Midwest ranked first in so-called "education deserts," with the deep south second (Hillman, & Weichman, 2016).

Unemployment, drug addiction, and a lack of health insurance are all too common in these education deserts. Vance (2016) noted the obstacles and barriers to educational opportunities as he was raised in one of these drug addicted, underemployed, and uninsured education deserts; yet, he received a scholarship to Yale Law School that granted him an opportunity to graduate education away from home. Vance (2016) became a critical voice on political media platforms during the 2016 presidential campaign explaining how current President Donald Trump was winning the support of education desert populations inhabited by many people who felt they had been prohibited from education and economic achievement.

Health & Lifestyle

Health and lifestyle are directly impacted by socioeconomic status. In 2016, 28.1 million Americans were without health insurance coverage, ranging from 16.6% uninsured in Texas to a low of 2.5% in Massachusetts (Barnett, Edward, & Berchick, 2016). Hispanics had the highest uninsured rate at 16.0%, Blacks 10.5 percent, Asians 7.6 percent, and non-Hispanic whites had the lowest uninsured rate at 6.3 percent (Barnett et al., 2016). Neighborhood quality is significant to health quality, and residents living in areas adjacent to junkyards, industrial factories, and high traffic areas are exposed to chemicals that impact health (Rothstein, 2017). Historically, zoning laws permitted toxic industrial and entertainment industries to flourish in low-income communities. Liquor stores, nightclubs, strip clubs, and hazardous occupations are in abundance in low-socioeconomic neighborhoods. Junkyards bring tons of toxic fumes into the atmosphere and kids play in these conditions for years. As a result, children develop asthma and other chronic illnesses and, if a family is uninsured and lack the resources to properly treat the condition, this can affect a student becoming truant (Rothstein, 2017). Discriminatory practices in housing ownership have always been a factor in the fabric of America socioeconomics and have consequences on low-socioeconomic communities.

Flint, Michigan. The Flint Michigan water system lead contamination is a recent high-profile example of the important public health disparities in lower socioeconomic communities. In 2012, Michigan state officials announced a new pipeline design for Flint, Michigan (Campbell, Greenberg, Mankikar, & Ross, 2016). In 2014, the project took a disastrous turn and caused a health crisis when the engineers, public works, water quality, public health and other officials failed to correct the water system after unsafe lead levels were detected in the city's water and in children's blood (Campbell et al., 2016). Elevated lead levels in children can impact neurological functioning, exposure may cause immediate poisoning, and the long-term effects such as hypertension, kidney damage, behavioral disturbance or loss of intellectual function may lay dormant for years before surfacing (Campbell et al., 2016). Flint state officials' decision to limit costs of remediation rather than protecting the residents, especially children, was an injustice that mostly affected low socioeconomic populations.

The health damage caused by the Flint, Michigan water crisis was studied by a community-based component of the health surveillance system in Genesee County, Michigan to examine the connection, if any, between household tap water quality and post-traumatic stress disorder (PTSD) (Kruger, Cupal, Franzen, Kodjebacheva, Bailey, Key, & Kaufman, 2017). After the study of 786 participants, those who experienced poorer tap water quality during the crisis experienced greater PTSD symptomatology (Kruger et al., 2017). Several Michigan officials were charged with involuntary manslaughter in connection with conditions that killed 12 people during the crisis (Gamin, 2017). On April 6, 2018, Governor Snyder announced that the free bottled water program would be ending as the water quality had been restored (Chavez, 2018). This had been part of the $450 million state and federal aid package that had been put into place (Chavez, 2018).

Home Environment

Parents are often the first teacher of children and when compelled to work numerous jobs to pay their bills, and left with little extra time, parents of low socioeconomic status struggle with guiding their children's engagement in school. This can result in children developing habits that exclude mastering the education curriculum (Kroll, 2012; Quane, Wilson, & Hwang, 2013). As with a lack of physical nutrition, mental undernutrition is problematic for brain development, and significantly impacts children in the early development stages when they are building the fundamentals of comprehension and understanding needed in school and life-long learning (Fernald & Weisleder, 2015).

Parental Engagement

The American population is multicultural with varying cultural norms in parenting philosophies, styles and strategies and home environments. Parental engagement is critical to children's learning, and parenting is more difficult under conditions of poverty (Zilberstein, 2016). Parenting styles vary between families depending on socioeconomic status; however, low socioeconomic parenting often includes discipline, strict rules, and instruction (Zilberstein, 2016). Neil deGrasse Tyson, astrophysicist, author, and science communicator, offered this in response to families who stifle a child's natural inquisitiveness

> *I'm often asked by parents what advice can I give them to help get kids interested in science? And I have only one bit of advice. Get out of their way. Kids are born curious. Period. I don't care about your economic background. I don't care what town you're born in, what city, what country. If you're a child, you are curious about your environment. You're overturning rocks. You're plucking leaves off of trees and petals off of flowers, looking inside, and you're doing things that create disorder in the lives of the adults around you. And then so what do adults do? They say, "Don't pluck the petals off the flowers. I just spent money on that. Don't play with the egg. It might break. Don't.... Everything is a don't. We spend the first year teaching them to walk and talk and the rest of their lives telling them to shut up and sit down* (YouTube, 2013).

Many parents cannot afford the cost or the time and space to allow children to safely explore and discover in their homes and neighborhoods, schools, and enrichment activities. Without such experiences, limitations in cognitive development may be exacerbated; however, their addition, if available, brings practical application to education concepts.

Final Thoughts

Income, education, and occupation are socioeconomic factors that have significant effects on parenting styles, home environment, language acquisition, school influence, and health, all of which impact children's development and learning. Early learning occurs at home through verbal interactions with parents that stimulate children's word recognition and use, which are critical to future learning. Having the wherewithal to purchase supplemental educational resources, such as digital devices, software, internet access, tutors, and summer academic camps, are benefits unavailable to all socioeconomic classes. The absence of reading practice and materials result in a precipitous decrease in learning gained at school.

Neighborhood quality affects learning as high-socioeconomic communities provide better spaces for children to explore and play in safer environments than do low-socioeconomic communities that have higher levels of pollution and threats of physical violence. Children in poor neighborhoods often enter schools poorly prepared to learn and attend schools ill-suited to meet their needs. As a result, the cycle of poverty is perpetuated. It is common to hear that those who have descended from generational poverty should improve their situations through education and diligence; yet, it is not that simple a task. In the case of children born into low socioeconomic families, the factors that matter in their development and impact their lifelong learning are stacked against them. Money means prestige and does matter for all children.

Points to Remember

- *Socioeconomic factors including income, education, occupation, parenting styles, home environment, language acquisition, school influence, health, and neighborhood quality have a tremendous impact on child development and learning.*
- *Starting at 18 months, children from high socioeconomic families developed essential learning skills from high verbal engagement early in their home environments, while those in low socioeconomic settings have a 30-million-word gap in language that can have a lifelong learning impact.*
- *Low socioeconomic neighborhoods consist of toxic pollutants that result in health risks for children who play in these environments.*
- *Areas in the country where post-secondary education institutions do not exist are known as an education desert. These rural populations experience high-drug addiction, low educational attainment, and health problems exacerbated by uninsured status.*
- *Social inequality has impacted social mobility for under-privileged and oppressed communities resulting in high*

percentages of group members living in poverty and experiencing the effects of low socioeconomic status on learning.

References

American Psychological Association. (2018). *Measuring socioeconomic status and subjective social status.* Retrieved from https://www.apa.org/pi/ses/resources/class/measuring-status.aspx

Barnett, J.C. & Berchick, E.R. (2016). *Health insurance coverage in the United States: Current population reports.* Retrieved from https://www.census.gov/content/dam/Census/library/publications/2017/demo/p60-260.pdf

Belasco, A. (2013). Creating College Opportunity: School Counselors and Their Influence on Postsecondary Enrollment. *Research in Higher Education, 54*(7), 781-804. DOI:10.1007/s11162-013-9297-4

Bowers, L.M. & Schwarz, I. (2018) Preventing Summer Learning Loss: Results of a Summer Literacy Program for Students from Low-SES Homes. *Reading & Writing Quarterly, 34*(2), 99-116. DOI: 10.1080/10573569.2017.1344943

Bristol, T. (2014). *Black men of the classroom: An exploration of how the organizational conditions, characteristics, and dynamics in schools affect black male teachers' pathways into the profession, experiences, and retention* (Doctoral dissertation). ProQuest Dissertations and Theses database (Order No. 3620206).

Brown, S. & Fischer. K. (2017). A Dying Town. *Chronicle of Higher Education.* Retrieved from https://www.chronicle.com/interactives/public-health

Campbell, C., Greenberg, R., Mankikar, D., & Ross, R. (2016). A Case Study of Environmental Injustice: The Failure in Flint. *International Journal of Environmental Research and Public Health, 13*(10), 951. http://doi.org/10.3390/ijerph13100951

Carson, C. (2001). *The Autobiography of Martin Luther King, Jr.* Hachette UK.

Carson, C. & Holloran, P. (2000). *A knock at midnight: Inspiration from the great sermons of Reverend Martin Luther King, Jr.* New York, NY: Warner

Chavez, N. (2018). Michigan will end Flint's free bottled water program. Retrieved from https://www.cnn.com/2018/04/07/us/flint-michigan-water-bottle-program-ends/index.html

Cheng, T.L., Johnson, S.B., & Goodman, E. (2016). Breaking the intergenerational cycle of disadvantage: The three generation approach. *Pediatrics, 137*(6), e20152467. Retrieved from https://www.ncbi.nlm.nih.gov/pmc/articles/PMC4894258/

Crosnoe, R., Purtell, K.M., Davis-Kean, P., Ansari, A., & Benner, A.D. (2016). *Developmental Psychology, 52*(4), 599-612. DOI: 10.1037/dev0000101

Emdin, C. (2017). *For white folks who teach in the hood..and the rest of y'all too: Reality pedagogy, and urban education.* Boston, MA: Beacon Press

Fernald, A., & Weisleder, A. (2015). Twenty Years after "Meaningful Differences," It's Time to Reframe the "Deficit" Debate about the Importance of Children's Early Language Experience. *Human Development, 58*(1), 1-4. DOI: 10.1159/000375515

Ganim, S. (2017). *Michigan officials charged in Flint Legionnaires' outbreak.* Retrieved from https://www.cnn.com/2017/06/14/health/flint-water-crisis-legionnaires-manslaughter-charges/index.html

Golinkoff, R.M., Hoff, E., Rowe, M., Tamis-LeMonda, C., & Hirsh-Pasek, K. (2018). *Talking with children matters: Defending the 30 million word gap.* Retrieved from https://www.brookings.edu/blog/education-plus-development/2018/05/21/defending-the-30-million-word-gap-disadvantaged-children-dont-hear-enough-child-directed-words/

Hart, B., & Risley, T.R. (1995). Meaningful differences in the everyday experience of young American children. Baltimore, MD: Brookes.

Hillman, N. & Weichman, T. (2016). *Education deserts: The continued significance of "place" In the twenty-first century.* Retrieved from https://www.acenet.edu/news-room/Documents/Education-Deserts-The-Continued-Significance-of-Place-in-the-Twenty-First-Century.pdf

Kroll, A. (2012). What we don't talk about when we talk about jobs: The continuing scandal of African-American joblessness. *New Labor Forum 21*(1), 48-55.

Kruger, D., Cupal, S., Franzen, S., Kodjebacheva, G., Bailey, E., Key, K., & Kaufman, M. M. (2017). Toxic trauma: Household water quality experiences predict posttraumatic stress disorder symptoms during the Flint, Michigan, water crisis. *Journal of Community Psychology, 45*(7), 957-962. https://doi.org/10.1002/jcop.21898

Martens, P.J., Chateau, D.G., Burlan, E.M.J., Finlayson, G.S., Smith, M.J., Taylor, C.R. ... & the PATHS Equity Team. (2014). The effect of neighborhood socioeconomic status on education and health outcomes for children living in social housing. *American Journal of Public Health, 104*(11), 2103-2113. DOI: 10.2015/AJPH.2014.302133

Myers, B. (2018). Who lives in education deserts? More people than you think. *The Chronicle of Higher Education.* Retrieved from https://www.chronicle.com/interactives/education-deserts

Otto, B. (2017). *Language Development in early childhood education* (5th ed.). New York, NY: Pearson

Quane, J., Wilson, W., & Hwang, J. (2013). The urban job crisis: Paths toward employment for low-income black and Latinos. *Harvard Magazine,* 24-26. Retrieved from *https://scholar.harvard.edu/jackelynhwang/publications/urban-jobs-crisis-paths-toward-employment-low-income-blacks-and-latinos*

Rock, C. (1997). *Rock This!* New York: Hyperion.

Rothstein, R. (2017). *The color of law: A Forgotten History of How Our Government Segregated America.* New York, NY: Liveright.

Semega, J., Fontenot, K., & Kollar, M. (2017). *Income and Poverty in the United States: Current population reports.* Retrieved from https://www.census.gov/content/dam/Census/library/publications/2017/demo/P60-259.pdf

Shapiro, T. M. (2004). *The hidden cost of being African American: How wealth perpetuates inequality.* New York, NY: Oxford University Press.

Vance, J. (2016). *Hillbilly elegy.* New York, NY: HarperCollins.

Young, N.D., Michael, C.N., & Jean, E. (2019). *From Dog Tags to Diploma: Understanding and Addressing the Educational Needs of Servicemembers and their Families.* Madison, IL: Atwood.

YouTube. (2013). *A message from a physicist to parents - Neil DeGrasse Tyson.* Retrieved from https://www.youtube.com/watch?v=vNHtfbKYPu8

Zahed Zahedani, Z., Rezaee, R., Yazdani, Z., Bagheri, S. & Nabeiei, P. (2016). The influence of parenting style on academic achievement and career path. *Journal of Advances in Medical Education Professionalism, 4*(3), 130-134. Retrieved from https://www.ncbi.nlm.nih.gov/pmc/articles/PMC4927255/pdf/jamp-4-130.pdf

Zilberstein, K. (2016). Parenting in families of low socioeconomic status: A review with implications for child welfare practice. *Family Court Review, 54*(2), 221-231. DOI: 10.1111/fcre.12222

Chapter Five

Religious Practices in the Classroom: Understanding and Honoring the Differences

Nicholas D. Young, *American International College*

Haley Scott, *American International College*

Throughout the course of history, there has been a strong influence of certain religious practices as implemented within public school systems across the United States. Judeo-Christian religious influences were openly highlighted and mainstreamed into common daily practice (Thomas, 2007). These secular religious origins can be dated back to the late 1800s and continued throughout the early 1960s, as the Civil Rights movement was launched (Diamond, 2008). Artifacts that exclusively represented Christian religious belief adorned the hallways of public schools, such as the Lord's Prayer, as well as a Christian-based opening prayer being encouraged for daily morning participation (Thomas, 2007). The influence of Christianity was also seen in Christian holidays being recognized within the public school calendars and their practices being celebrated and implemented within the school systems (Diamond, 2008).

Meanwhile, other symbols were put into everyday practice and implemented for non-Christian school children. Through this inclusive practice, other religious denominations were left to mirror their practices and acculturation for this diverse group of students within the public school classroom. This adaptation to the dominant was assimilated in their culture and religiosity among minorities is known as psychological dexterity (Dantley, 2005). Asian, Hispanic, and African-American communities have utilized their spirituality as a safe haven in which to express their repressed self-identity, religion and culture (Dantley, 2005).

What once was a silent minority of diversity within the American classroom shifted with an influx of immigration to the United States. This led to vast multicultural changes within the classroom today. A 2009 study estimated that "23% of children in the United States under 10 come from immigrant families" (Sirin, Ryce, & Mir, 2009, p. 463). Previously, in the Progressive Era of the early 1900s, the non-Christian population only encompassed a very small percentage; however, in 1995 it tripled and now includes, "Hindus, Jews, Muslims, Black Muslims, Buddhists, Chinese-folk religionists, Sikhs and Tribal-religions" (Thomas, 2007, p. 54). This rapid growth was a catalyst for systematic change, which helped mold and shape the landscape that was once predominately Christian.

Over the past decade, since the religious shift and the budding multicultural classroom, the doors opened for various other religious affiliations to openly practice outside of the classroom (Thomas, 2007). This shift, according to Romanowki and Talbert (2000), had a significant impact on the role and shape of religion within America and within the classroom itself. This significant change to the "melting pot" of America was not consistently documented within U.S history and within all public school systems. Moreover, pedagogically it was not represented in children's textbooks and curricula; thus, diversity was not truly reflected in the classroom (Young, 2010).

With the turn of the century, "eight out of ten people worldwide are affiliated with a specific religious group" (Brooks, 2017, p. 646). Later, the civil rights movement was the pinnacle in creating advocacy for the separation of church and state and the U.S Supreme Court was instrumental in prohibiting religious artifacts such as prayer in the classroom after a court case in 1962 (Longley, 2018). It is projected that by 2042, the minority population will drastically increase and, therefore, transcend into the majority population (Suh & Samuel, 2011). Likewise, there will be an increase in minority children, including more than 44 percent in 2050 (Suh & Samuel, 2011). Today's classroom, therefore, encompasses a variety of cultures and religious beliefs.

The religious landscape of the classroom has diversified over the course of history, yet it is still challenging to present the topic for conversation without engendering some strong opinions (Shahjahan, 2010). It is vital, therefore, to thoroughly cover the pedagogical value and importance in understanding and incorporating students' various religious makeup within the classroom and learning environment.

The Interconnection Between Early Childhood and Religion

Fred Rogers, a social justice pioneer from the acclaimed early childhood television show, Mr. Rogers Neighborhood, set the precedent for public television programming and public sectors, such as public school systems, to open the door for social justice issues (Buchanan & Baumgartner, 2010). These included the role of diversity in the classroom and allowing religion back into the fabric of learning and within the classroom environment (Buchanan & Baumgartner, 2010). Rogers and early childhood researchers saw the pedagogical value of meshing both the school and home environment and the significant difference that was made within the learning environment during those key early years (Lietz, 2014; Kamenetz, 2018; Young, 2010). When a cultural congruence, which includes religion, is present between teachers, child, and parents, this is favorable for the child's long-term educational and socioemotional growth; thus, a parallel process between all parties becomes emergent (Agirdag, Merry, & Van Houtte, 2016).

Cultural and Religious Coherence in the Classroom

As indicated by Regnerus, Smith & Fritsch (2003), religion as a whole has a direct correlation to positive adolescent outcomes. It serves as a protective factor for many minority and immigrant adolescent populations against drug and alcohol use and abuse, while reducing the incidence of depression (Regnerus et al., 2003). Molock, Puri, Matlin, and Barkside (2006) highlight that for African-Americans, religiosity fosters healthy social and emotional development, promotes baseline regulation, and assists in building healthy coping skills. A study from Greening and Stoppelbein (2002), indicated that religion served as a deterrent to suicidal ideations and that this specific population participates in significantly more religious practices than any other population that they studied. This research suggests that the incorporation of religion into the learning environment for this group is key for overall fundamental success.

It is recommended that educators have a general understanding of students' culture and religious beliefs they will follow in the public school environment. This not only displays a general empathetic understanding but models this behavior to the classroom to be replicated among their peers. A longitudinal study of immigrant families and teachers found that when there is a misunderstanding among teachers as to their immigrant students' cultural and religious beliefs, this may affect their learning environment (Rogers-Sirin, Ryce, & Sirin, 2014). A miscommunication may lead to the teacher misreading the cues related to the child's instructional capabilities, test placement, social and emotional engagement, and behavioral components within the classroom setting (Ilosvay, 2016).

As Buchanan and Baumgartner (2010) allude, researchers also highlight the importance of incorporating religion within the classroom during the early childhood years as it helps to develop a "sense of belonging, respect for their self and others and an awareness and appreciation of the unknown" for the child (p. 91). A necessary next step, therefore, is to discuss specific examples that have been widely researched in regard to cultural and religious coherence within the classroom.

African American

Religion within the African American community has been seen as a catalyst of hope. W.E.B. DuBois (as cited in Diamond 2008) highlighted that religion had been a "means of survival," (p. 92) since the inception of slavery and the deeply rooted segregation practices that transpired in the classroom and within their communities. In 1950, the Topeka National Association for the Advancement of Colored People launched a first of its kind lawsuit challenging an 1879 law that allowed segregated schools (Thomas, 2007). Later, in 1954, the U.S Supreme court got involved when Caucasian communities defended their rights, per se, for African Americans to remain in segregated schools and not commingle within their communities; this group argued that civil rights were not being violated (Thomas, 2007). The spark of the Civil Rights movement instituted a glimpse of hope for desegregation within society and in school systems across the country and opened the door for other religious practices to be seen and heard within the public school systems (Thomas, 2007).

Moreover, during this period, one of the most well-known Christian African-American pastors and leaders of our time, Dr. Martin Luther King, Jr. led this pursuit of equal rights (A&E Television, 2018). Years later, there is a remembrance of racism, which still lingers within the shadows of past policies such as No Child Left Behind and non-lateral educational funding for highly oppressed communities of color (Klein, 2015). During the time period of Dr. King and still today, members of the African-American community find solace from within the safety net of the Black church. Behind the church walls, specific practices are deeply rooted within their past and present heritage to include Bible studies, Sunday school, praise and worship, liturgical dance, and youth mentoring programs for academic excellence (Diamond, 2008). Additionally, as Mattis and Jagers (2001) further explain, mission work performed within the church walls and out in the African-American community includes "visiting the sick, and shut-in, feeding the poor and elderly" (p. 530).

African Americans' religious affiliations encompass a wide range of religious doctrines across the United States. These include African-American Christianity, Jehovah's Witnesses, as well as Rastafarian, Baptist, Methodist, Pentecostal, and many other denominations (Pew Research Center, 2018). One common, key feature of African-American faith communities, as Hubbard, Hatfield, and Santucci (2007) point out, is their freedom of expression during their church services. This may include hands being raised to signify oneness with God, or many times a more soulful music choice being sung during services.

An example of an African-American holiday that holds deep significance is Kwanzaa, which is centered on celebrating seven days of specific virtues: "unity, self-determination, collective work, and responsibility, cooperative economics, purpose, creativity and faith" (Hubbard et al., 2007, p. 42).

Islamic Faith and Practices

In the United States, the Islamic faith is comprised of a very diverse group of people to include immigrants from Asia, Africa, and Middle Eastern counties, along with others in the United States that have converted to this faith (Carolan, Bagherinia, Juhari, Himelright, & Mouton-Sanders, 2000). Muslim Americans are one of the fastest growing religious populations throughout the United States today, although there is still a lingering stereotype associated with their culture, identity, and faith, post-911 (Hodge, 2002; Ilosvay, 2016; Lebowitz, 2016). This hidden bias, known as *Islamophobia*, can be attributed to a misunderstanding of their attire, mannerisms, and faith (Gallup, 2018). In fact, in 2005, Muslim parents from a high school in Texas took their school district to court to fight for their children's right to exercise private student prayer throughout the school day (Thomas, 2007). In the Muslim faith, prayer is performed up to five times throughout the day. As James, Schweber, Kunzman, Barton, and Logan (2015) attest, throughout the course of history in the United States, Muslims have endured similar prejudices and marginalization that members of other religious affiliations (such as Catholics and Jews) experienced. This misunderstanding and lack of accommodations for others' cultural and religious beliefs is not only felt within the United States but worldwide and with various religious denominations as well; for example, in France, a Muslim elementary school child was not allowed to wear her head scarf, or *hijab*, in school nor were Christians allowed to show their crosses around their necks (Ilosvay, 2016).

It is vital that educators understand the cultural and religious beliefs of their students. In the case of the Muslim population, teachers should strive for further understanding of some of the general practices of their faith. This would include adhering to a strict diet that prohibits any pork products, which although it tends not to be required until their adolescent years, is often encouraged by their parents starting at a younger age (Sirin, Ryce, & Mir, 2009). Another area to note is that Muslim students during physical education are not allowed to participate in gym classes that include both genders; this practice is associated with their prayer services, in which each gender is separated into a different room. In this particular faith, they celebrate their day of service on Fridays and their higher power is associated with the five pillars from Allah and Muhammad is his messenger (Gallup, 2018). Their written word is known as the Qur'an and some of the Muslim holidays that they hold sacred include Eid al-Fitr and Eid al-Adha (Gallup, 2018).

Jehovah's Witnesses

The Jehovah's Witnesses have origins that date back from the late 1800s to the early 1900s. One of this religion's early organizers was Charles Taze Russell (Thomas, 2007). This religion does not refer to itself as a specific domination but rather a society of people who congregate in institutions called Kingdom Halls. They are also regionalized into sub-factors known as circuits and one specific pastor does not lead each circuit; rather, each is represented by a group of appointed elders and a circuit overseer (Thomas, 2007). Each congregant is expected to perform service work in the community by distributing recruitment literature. The goal, based on their belief, is to prepare themselves and others for the last days.

It is important for educators to note that although Jehovah's Witnesses do participate in funerals, weddings, or elections, in a classroom setting they cannot celebrate or participate in any class group celebrations such as birthdays, nor can they salute the flag (Martinson, 2008). Throughout history, Jehovah's Witnesses have initiated more fundamental constitutional cases to protect their civil liberties and religious beliefs, such as not saluting the flag (Martinson, 2008). One of the first lawsuits to test this breach of a civil liberty was the Billy Gobitis case in 1935 (Thomas, 2007). This case was brought about because two Jehovah's Witness children from Minersville, Pennsylvania were expelled for not saluting the flag (Bill of Rights Institute, 2018). All but one judge agreed with the school district; however, three years later, a similar case was heard and the original case was overturned as the judges believed that this was a constitutional violation (Bill of Rights Institute, 2018; Martinson, 2008).

Christianity in the Twenty-First Century

The Christian population, over 290 million people, spans a wide spectrum of denominational affiliations within the United States (Thomas, 2007). The Christian population can be grouped into two distinct categories, fundamentalists and moderates, while Christian denominations fall into the following categories "Protestant 57%, Roman Catholic 21%, and other Christian 6.4%" (Thomas, 2007, p. 70). Hubbard et al. (2007) share that Fundamentalists further divide into conservative, evangelical or Pentecostal Christians, and moderate or non-doctrine Christians. The three other main sub-groups of Christianity include the Eastern Orthodox, Roman Catholic, and Protestant branches (Hubbard et al., 2007). Eastern Orthodoxy is associated with traditions from Europe, while the Roman Catholics look to the Pope for guidance and direction. Roman Catholics comprise the largest subset of Christians today (Thomas, 2007). Earlier in history, as Thomas (2007) shares, the Protestant denominations, broke away from the Catholic church and today are categorized into "Anglicans, Episcopalians, Baptists, Lutherans, Methodists and Presbyterians" (p. 74).

The Latino and Hispanic populations traditionally have had strong affiliations to the various Christian religious dominations. Religion within the Latino culture plays a significant role within the fundamental educational success of Latino children (Brinig & Garnett, 2014). Recent studies have shown that for Latino children from impoverished neighborhoods, religion practice within a classroom setting creates an external cohesiveness with children from other cultures (Brinig & Garnett, 2014). Within the Latino culture, religion is deeply integrated in other modern traditions that began when Latinos migrated in the early 1960s (Sirin, Ryce, & Mir, 2009). These include celebrating Three Kings Day, or as many Latino Christians refer to it, the Feast of Epiphany, that celebrates Jesus and the three wise men who traveled from afar to adorn him with gifts; and a *quinceanera*, otherwise known as a sweet fifteen, which is a celebration in honor of the child taking the next step from childhood into the teenage years on her fifteenth birthday. There is a Catholic mass honoring this celebration following a gathering with family and friends.

Judaism

Throughout history, across the United States and abroad, many religions have been ostracized for their beliefs; however, through adversity, there has also been resiliency, which is abundant within the various religious communities and magnifies healing from within; this is projected outwards towards other marginalized groups. The Jewish community is one of many religious groups that speaks this common language of hope and perseverance (Urkin, Fram, Jotkowitz, & Naimer, 2017).

The Jewish religion is reflective of one primary God and asks its congregants to follow a specific lifestyle, beliefs, and commandments according to the Torah Urkin et al., 2017). Services are held at the synagogue; yet, one pronounced difference between differing religious factions is that Jews do not tend to verbalize about their faith (Urkin et al., 2017). Some important holidays that the Jews follow include: Rosh Hashanah, Yom Kippur and Passover. Children tend not to attend school on these days as well. Also, entry into adulthood is recognized and celebrated by a Bar Mitzvah for boys and a Bat Mitzvah for girls (Hubbard et al., 2007).

The Jewish community is a cohesive group that utilizes its support systems from within their insular communities, especially for traditional Orthodox Jews; yet, there are also more reformed Jews who are more liberal in their beliefs and congregate with people outside of their faith (Urkin et al., 2017). A Yiddish proverb noted from Diamant (2007) defines this practice best as, "Life is with people" (p. 94). This proverb captures the essence of why it is important to embrace the Jewish culture, connect and be surrounded by others from within the community. As, Urkin et al. (2017) assert, today in the United States Jewish children are often tri-lingual and fully immersed in English, as well as the common language of their host country, to include Jewish households speaking Yiddish or Hebrew. Many observant Jewish American homes are also inclusive of a kosher lifestyle (Diamant, 2007). This typically means that only kosher meat is brought into the household, specific food groups can or cannot be eaten together, cooking pans and other items are used separately. This is part of the body of laws known as *kashrut*; therefore, if a child in a classroom is "keeping" kosher, it is vital that the educator asks about the magnitude of their dietary restrictions (Diamant, 2007).

Buddhism

The late 1960s were a pinnacle time period, as Buddhism and other Asian-influenced religions such as Hinduism and Taoism migrated into the once homogenous classrooms throughout the United States (Thomas, 2007). Sanctions had been lifted and Asian immigrants entered the United States sharing their cultural and religious beliefs with American culture. Buddhism is one of the largest religions practiced within the United States and is comprised of mostly Asian Americans (Lizardi & Gearing, 2009).

In Buddhism, the *yana* is equivalent to their doctrine. There are three sub-types of Buddhism to include *Theravada, Mahayana, and Vajrayana* and "Theravada, is linked to teaching of the elders, Mahayana is the universal vehicle and Vajrayana is the Apocalyptic vehicle" (Thomas, 2007, p. 9). All of the Buddhist traditions, however, examine internal suffering and how to conquer the discourse associated with them from within (Thomas, 2007).

Notably, there have been numerous studies that found a direct correlation between one of the techniques utilized in Buddhist practice, mindfulness, and various outcomes. Mindfulness, according to Ergas (2014), was first conceptualized in the 1800s based on Eastern (Buddhist) philosophy. Later in the 1970s, Jon Kabat-Zinn, a Buddhist, introduced the concept of mindfulness meditation practice to assist hospital patients in reducing their stress levels (Ergas, 2014). In conjunction with Kabat-Zinn, the University of Massachusetts opened a Mindfulness clinic, the first of its kind in the country (Ergas, 2014). Mindfulness helps a person learn how to deal with stressful situations and self-regulate in order get back to baseline (Keng, Smoski, & Robins, 2011). This practice overall helps calm and soothe the person internally.

Various school systems across the country today have begun utilizing Buddhist practices and principles by integrating them into behavior modification programs in classrooms. These principles do not promote a religious standpoint; rather, they are being used to teach children a skill set in regard to self-regulation through meditative practices (Mindful Schools, 2018). In fact, according to Mendelson and colleagues (2010), there is evidence, from various studies conducted with low-income students, that shows significant improvements in self-actualization, and increases in distress tolerance skills. In 1987, the California school system was the first to institute a multicultural precedent for other school districts across the nation by revising the history books to incorporate various aspects of Hinduism and Buddhism into the literature (Brown, 2008).

It is important in a classroom setting to not have a stereotypical viewpoint about Buddhism, and not place them into one specific category. Not all Buddhists, for example, incorporate meditation practices into their daily rituals, nor are all of them vegetarians, although many are (Hubbard et al., 2007). It is important, therefore, for teachers to check in with the family about any dietary restrictions for the child, as well. Some of the holidays that Buddhists observe include *Wesak* (the birth of Buddha), and *Ulambana* or *Obon*, which takes place in late summer and includes a food offering to ancestors. Another holiday celebrated by some Buddhists is *Songkran*, which is the Thai New Year (Religion Facts, 2018).

Final Thoughts

As indicated by Regnerus et al. (2003), religion as a whole has a direct correlation to positive adolescent outcomes. It serves as a protective factor for many minorities and immigrant adolescent populations, against drug and alcohol use and abuse, while reducing incidents of depression. For minority children, religiosity further fosters social and emotional development, promotes baseline emotion regulation and assists in building healthy coping skills (Molock et al., 2006). Religion also serves as a deterrent to suicide; therefore, overall, the incorporation of religion into the learning environment for students of faith is key for their fundamental success throughout their school journey (Lizardi & Gearing, 2009; Molock et al., 2006).

It is vital to take into consideration the diversified classroom and that it is pedagogically reflective of the entire student body; therefore, when planning extra-curricular activities for students, the teacher must be reminded to not only honor Christian holiday schedules but other denominations and religions as well, such as Muslim students fasting for Ramadan or a Jewish student attending a service at a mosque on a Friday afternoon or evenings (James et al., 2015). Educators must be purposeful and have a high level of sensitivity in the verbiage that they use, ensuring that it is welcoming to all students and families. Finally, one should take into consideration that "the silencing of the spiritual voice through privileging the academic voice is increasingly being drowned out by the empathetic chorus of those whose underlying versions of truth cry out, we are spiritual people' (Dillard, et al., p. 98).

Points to Remember

- *Provide a culturally attuned learning environment: The school environment, curriculum and holiday and academic schedule should not be monoculture, but rather represent the diversity of your school.*
- *Foster cultural congruence: When a cultural congruence, which includes religion, is present between teachers, child, and parents, this is favorable for the child's long-term educational and socioemotional growth.*
- *Practice reflective modeling: It is recommended that educators have a general understanding of students' culture and religious beliefs. This not only displays a general empathetic understanding but models this behavior to the classroom to then be replicated among their peers.*

- *Transformative pedagogy:* Early childhood researchers have seen the pedagogical value of meshing both the school and home environment to the significant difference that it makes within the palpable learning environment during the key early years.
- *The integration of religion fosters positive long-term outcomes for children:* Religion as a whole has a direct correlation to positive adolescent outcomes. It serves as a protective factor for many minority and immigrant adolescent populations against drug and alcohol use and abuse, while reducing the incidence of depression.
- *Looking glass self:* It is vital to remain an objective facilitator when fostering conversations about religion within a classroom setting.
- *Create and cultivate collaborative partnerships:* Parents, teachers, students and the community play a key role in building and sustaining healthy partnerships that encourage religious dialogue.

References

A&E Television. (2018). *Martin Luther King, Jr.* Retrieved from https://www.history.com/topics/black-history/martin-luther-king-jr

Agirdag, O., Merry, M.S., & Van Houtte, M. (2016). Teachers' understanding of multicultural education and the correlates of multicultural content integration in Flanders. *Education and Urban Society, 48*(6), 556-582. DOI: 10.1177/0013124514536610

Buchanan, T.K. & Baumgartner, J.J. (2010). Supporting each child's spirit. *Young Children, 65*(2), 173-184. 90-93. Retrieved from https://www.researchgate.net/publication/266912249_Supporting_each_child's_spirit

Bill of Rights Institute. (2018). *Minersville school district v. Gobitis (1940)*. Retrieved from https://billofrightsinstitute.org/educate/educator-resources/lessons-plans/landmark-supreme-court-cases-elessons/minersville-school-district-v-gobitis-1940/

Brinig, M. F. & Garnett, N.S. (2014). *Lost classroom, lost community: Catholic schools' importance in urban America.*

Brooks, M. C. (2017). Southern Filipino school leaders and religious diversity: A typology. *International Journal of Educational Management, 31*(5), 646-660. DOI:10.1108/ijem-08-2016-0164

Brown, S. (2008). *A Buddhist in the classroom.* Albany, NY: State University of New York Press.

Carolan, M., Bagherinia, G., Juhari, R., Himelright, J., & Mouton-Sanders, M. (2000). Contemporary Muslim families: Research and practice.

Contemporary Family Therapy, 11(1), 67-79. DOI: 10.1023/A:1007770532624

Dantley, M. E. (2005). African American spirituality and Cornel West's notions of prophetic pragmatism: Restructuring educational leadership in American urban schools. *Educational Administration Quarterly, 41*(4), 651-674. DOI:10.1177/0013161x04274274

Diamant, A., & Cooper, H. (2007). *Living a Jewish life: Jewish traditions, customs, and values for today's families.* New York, NY: HarperCollins.

Diamond, M. R. (2008). *Encountering faith in the classroom: Turning difficult discussions into constructive engagement.* Sterling, VA: Stylus Pub.

Ergas, O. (2014). Mindfulness in education at the intersection of science, religion, and healing. *Critical Studies in Education, 55*(1), 58-72. doi:10.1080/17508487.2014.858643

Gallup. (2018). *Islamophobia: Understanding anti-Muslim sentiment in the west.* Retrieved from https://news.gallup.com/poll/157082/islamophobia-understanding-anti-muslim-sentiment-west.aspx

Greening, L & Stoppelbein, L. (2002). Religiosity, attributional style, and social support as psychosocial buffers for African American and White adolescents' perceived risk for suicide. *Suicide and Life-Threatening Behavior, 32,* 404–417. [PubMed: 12501965]

Hodge, D. (2002). Working with Muslim youths: Understanding the values and beliefs of Islamic discourse. *Children & Schools, 24*(1), 6-20. DOI: 10.1093/cs/24.1.6

Hubbard, B. J., Hatfield, J. T., & Santucci, J. A. (2007). *An educator's classroom guide to America's religious beliefs and practices.* Westport, CT: Libraries Unlimited.

Ilosvay, K. (2016). Religion in schools? The importance of recognizing the impact of religious experiences. *The Journal of Faith, Education and Community, 1*(2), 1-28. Retrieved from https://scholarworks.sfasu.edu/cgi/viewcontent.cgi?article=1005&context=jfec

James, J. H., Schweber, S., Kunzman, R., Barton, K. C., & Logan, K. (2015). *Religion in the classroom: Dilemmas for democratic education.* New York, NY: Routledge.

Kamenetz, A. (2018). *How the science of learning is catching up to Mr. Rogers.* Retrieved from https://www.npr.org/2018/08/08/635354413/how-learning-science-is-catching-up-to-mr-rogers

Keng, S., Smoski, M. J., & Robins, C. J. (2011). Effects of mindfulness on psychological health: A review of empirical studies. *Clinical Psychology Review, 31*(6), 1041-1056. doi:10.1016/j.cpr.2011.04.006

Klein, A. (2015). *No child left behind: An overview.* Retrieved from https://www.edweek.org/ew/section/multimedia/no-child-left-behind-overview-definition-summary.html

Lebowitz, J. (2016, September). Muslim American youth in the post 9/11 public education system. Retrieved September 28, 2018, from https://cedar.wwu.edu/fairhaven_acscapstone/6/

Lietz, J. (2014). *A journey into the neighborhood: An analysis of Fred Rogers and his lessons for educational leaders.* Retrieved from https://ecommons.luc.edu/cgi/viewcontent.cgi?referer=https://www.google.com/&httpsredir=1&article=2096&context=luc_diss

Lizardi, D., & Gearing, R. E. (2009). Religion and suicide: Buddhism, Native American and African religions, Atheism, and Agnosticism. *Journal of Religion and Health, 49*(3), 377-384. doi:10.1007/s10943-009-9248-8

Longley, R. 92018). *School Prayer: Separation of church and state: Why Johnny can't pray—at school.* Retrieved from https://www.thoughtco.com/separation-of-church-and-state-3572154

Martinson, D. L. (2008). Using the Jehovah's Witness cases to stimulate student thinking. *The Social Studies, 99*(2), 77-82. DOI:10.3200/tsss.99.2.77-82

Mattis, J. S., & Jagers, R. J. (2001). A relational framework for the study of religiosity and spirituality in the lives of African Americans. *Journal of Community Psychology, 29*(5), 519-539. DOI:10.1002/jcop.1034

Mendelson, T., Greenberg, M. T., Dariotis, J. K., Gould, L. F., Rhoades, B. L., & Leaf, P. J. (2010). Feasibility and preliminary outcomes of a school-based mindfulness intervention for urban youth. *Journal of Abnormal Child Psychology, 38*(7), 985-994. DOI:10.1007/s10802-010-9418-x

Mindful Schools. (2018). *Research on mindfulness.* Retrieved from https://www.mindfulschools.org/about-mindfulness/research/

Molock, S. D., Puri, R., Matlin, S., & Barksdale, C. (2006). Relationship between religious coping and suicidal behaviors among African American adolescents. *Journal of Black Psychology, 32*(3), 366-389. doi:10.1177/0095798406290466

Pew Research Center. (2018). *Religious Landscape Study.* Retrieved from http://www.pewforum.org/religious-landscape-study/racial-and-ethnic-composition/black/

Regnerus, M., Smith, C., & Fritsch, M. (2003). Religion in the lives of American adolescents: A review of the literature. Retrieved from https://open.bu.edu/bitstream/handle/2144/6/litreview.pdf?sequence=1

Religion Facts. (2018). *Buddhist holidays and festivals.* Retrieved from http://www.religionfacts.com/buddhism/holidays

Rogers-Sirin, L., Ryce, P., & Sirin, S.R. (2014). Acculturation, acculturative stress, and cultural mismatch and their influences on immigrant children and adolescents' well-being. In R. Dimitrova et al. (ed.), Global Perspectives on Well-Being in Immigrant Families, pp. 11-30. New York, NY: Springer Science + Business Media

Romanowski, M.H. & Talbert, K.M. (2000). Addressing the influence of religion and faith in American history. *The Clearing House, 73*(3), 134-137. Retrieved from https://www.jstor.org/stable/30189522

Shahjahan, R. A. (2010). Toward a spiritual praxis: The role of spirituality among faculty of color teaching for social justice. *The Review of Higher Education, 33*(4), 473-512. DOI:10.1353/rhe.0.0166

Sirin, S. R., Ryce, P., & Mir, M. (2009). How teachers' values affect their evaluation of children of immigrants: Findings from Islamic and public schools. *Early Childhood Research Quarterly, 24*(4), 463-473. DOI: 10.1016/j.ecresq.2009.07.003

Suh, B.K. & Samuel, F.A. (2011). *New England Reading Association Journal, 47*(1). Retrieved from https://www.questia.com/library/journal/1P3-2478461901/the-value-of-multiculturalism-in-a-global-village

Thomas, R. M. (2007). *God in the classroom: Religion and America's public schools.* Lanham, MD: Rowman & Littlefield Education.

Urkin, J., Fram, E., Jotkowitz, A., & Naimer, S. A. (2017). Nurturing a society of learners: Suggestions from traditional Jewish pedagogy for medical education. *Rambam Maimonides Medical Journal, 8*(3). DOI: 10.5041/rmmj.10309

Young, E. (2010). Challenges to conceptualizing and actualizing culturally relevant pedagogy: How viable is the theory in classroom practice? *Journal of Teacher Education, 61*(3), 248-260. DOI:10.1177/0022487109359775

Chapter Six

Diverse Ability Levels: Differentiating Instruction to Teach to All Learners

Jacqueline Hawkins, *University of Houston*

Sara J. Jones, *University of Houston*

Kristi L. Santi, *University of Houston*

Today's effective teachers motivate students, help them to gain purpose or agency in their lives, focus their mindsets on lifelong success, and teach them reading, mathematics, science, and social studies (Ferguson, Phillips, Rowley, & Friedlander, 2015). For many members of the public, the knee-jerk reaction is that academics are the main focus of school. That is most likely because academics are the main outcomes that are measured and reported in the news; yet, there are other aspects of school that are, for the most part, not measured and published on an annual basis that are just as important, if not more so.

Research has demonstrated that effective teachers must engage a variety of other skills in support of the success of all learners. It is clear that students learn more from their teachers than academics; for example, the environment in which students learn, their engagement with educators, the responses that they get from adults, and how important students feel in a school environment are but a few of the considerations and 'educator messaging' activities that can make the difference in helping all learners (Tomlinson & Doubet, 2005). Educators are learning that it is more than differentiating the day-to-day instruction that relates to the academic content – it's about the context and the manner in which that differentiated instruction is delivered (Tomlinson & Doubet, 2005). The need for both differentiated instruction and attention to classroom, school, and district contexts will do much to address the achievement gaps.

The Achievement Gap Initiative (Ferguson et al., 2015), at Harvard University, has a mission to frame important issues that will help to bridge the gap between research and practice to promote excellence with equity. Academic disparities in schools lead to economic disparities in jobs and careers (Torraco, 2018). Disparities in early life can continue throughout school and impact the future of millions of children. The achievement gap formally begins in schools, yet it has far-reaching consequences for our society/children (Hansen, Levesque, Quintero, & Valant, 2018). If not addressed early, the gap widens. Educational research has provided the field with the skills to address the gap. When educators have the will to differentiate instruction and learning, create caring classrooms, and focus on social and emotional learning more students can excel, and the achievement gap shrinks. To achieve this outcome, educators must own their potential role in the achievement gap and then learn new tools to use as interventions to best support students.

The Path of the Educator into the Classroom

By the 21st century, many people believe that anybody can teach, that teaching requires little formal preparation, and that teacher education programs are unnecessary (Darling-Hammond, 2006). Instruction can be delivered at home through home schooling, in private schools where teachers may or may not be certified to teach, in schools where teachers have been alternatively certified and may have begun their careers without the requisite credentials, and by fully certified teachers (Darling-Hammond, 2006). Without proper training, teachers may lack the skills needed to reach the variation of children that enter their classrooms. Teachers must have the skills to ensure that all students learn – not just students for whom learning may come easily or students who come to school ready to learn. Teachers must have the skills to reach students who are considered by many to be the most difficult to teach – students who fail grades, students who have disabilities, students who can be disruptive in class, and students who don't seem motivated to engage with their own learning. It all begins with how teachers are prepared for the job (Auhl & Daniel, 2014).

Research on teacher preparation has identified three essential components (1) courses, course content, and clinical practice must be actively integrated throughout a program; (2) theory and practice must be linked through intense and on-going clinical supervision in practice; and, (3) relationships must be forged with diverse schools and campuses to ensure that teachers can develop and deliver effective instruction for all students (Darling-Hammond, 2006). All three practices must be evident if teachers are to be successful with all students. Teachers must not only know their academic content (the *what* of teaching) and how to teach (the *how* of teaching) but must know their students and their unique needs (the *who* they are teaching) (Darling-Hammond, 2006). Indeed, the Association of Teacher Education (2018) identifies that, while teaching is their first standard, cultural competence (applying cultural competence and promoting social justice in teacher education) is their second standard.

Cultural competence involves teachers first knowing their own culture and learning to understand and actively engage with other cultures – especially the indigenous cultures of the students in their classroom (Association of Teacher Education (2018). Teachers who engage in culturally relevant pedagogy learn that students from different cultures can achieve the highest expectations and that teachers must hold both themselves and their students accountable (Gay, 2005). They must learn about their own identity but also to learn about challenges and inequities that perpetuate in schools. In turn, this approach helps prepare them to support students from diverse backgrounds to excel both socially and academically (Gay, 2005).

Demographic Shifts in Classrooms

Educators have witnessed a dramatic shift in classroom demographics over just the last two decades (Musu-Gillette, De Brey, McFarland, Hussar, Sonnenberg, & Wilkinson-Flicker, 2017). While the number of school-aged children increased by approximately one million from 2000 to 2016, the racial and ethnic diversity of this age group is significant (Musu-Gillette et al., 2017). Specifically, the National Center for Education Statistics report that, as a percentage, White students decreased from 75.6 to 61.2 and for Black students there was a percentage increase from 11.8 to 12.4 students (Musu-Gillette et al., 2017). In this same time period, Hispanic and Asian students saw a greater projected percentage of growth with 9 and 2.8 respectively in 1990 to 17.8 and 5.6 percent in 2016 (Musu-Gillette et al., 2017). Children with multiracial backgrounds also grew from less than one percent reported to 2.4 percent during this time period (Snyder, De Brey, & Dillow, 2018).

Beyond racial and ethnic diversity, teachers are facing a student population with increasing social needs (Wells, Fox, Cordova-Cobo, 2016). This comes at a time when we as educators and researchers are more and more aware that a focus only on academics is not enough. A student's basic survival needs, learning differences, and social and emotional needs must be met in order for students to learn and achieve in schools. Between

2000 and 2016, the number of public school students who received need-based free or reduced lunch jumped from 38.3 percent to 52.1 percent (Musu-Gillette et al., 2017). During the same 16 year time period, students enrolled in English as a Second Languages instruction increased from 8.1 percent to 9.5 percent nationally, but several states saw rates much higher (Musu-Gillette et al., 2017). For instance, Kansas saw the highest increase from 3.2 percent to 10.2 percent, while Arizona dropped from 15.0 percent to 6.1 percent (Musu-Gillette et al., 2017). This differential impact is possibly due to the changing state policies on immigration and education. The number of students receiving special education services in 2006 jumped to 6.7 million students compared to only 3.7 million in 1976 (Planty et al., 2008). Additionally, in 2007 one study found that over two-thirds of students reported experiencing at least one traumatic incident by age 16, with 13.4 percent of those resulting in some post-traumatic stress symptoms (Copeland, Keeler, Angold, & Costello, 2007).

In a world where travel is more frequent and easier, where people move across borders and continents to realize career opportunities, and where war and oppression are the basis for asylum, the globalization of classrooms is increasingly the norm in the United States (Merriam & Bierema, 2014). It is impossible for teachers to share all cultural demographics and experiences with all students. In 2016, 80 percent of teachers were white, while only nine percent were Hispanic and seven percent Black (McFarland et al., 2018). As educators, however, we are responsible for understanding the differences that we may have from our students and working to remove any barriers that might exist between ourselves and our students, as well as amongst our students. Given the varied and extensive needs of school children in the United States, administrators must approach this issue holistically, ensuring that their teachers are equipped with the strategies and resources needed to reach every student where they are. The high rates of poverty and mental health issues put a strain on schools that may not be able to respond to these issues alone. Partnering with non-profits, community organizations, universities and local businesses are possible ways to address the resource gaps and care for students (Young, Jean, & Citro, 2018a; Young, Jean, & Citro, 2018b; Young, Jean, & Mead, 2018). Within the classrooms, differentiated instruction, creating caring classrooms, and equipping students with social and emotional skills have all been shown to increase student achievement across student demographics (Durlak, Weissberg, Dymnicki, Taylor & Schellinger, 2011; Young, Jean, & Citro, 2018a; Young, Jean, & Citro, 2018b).

A Pivotal Point

Diverse backgrounds, a variety of life experiences, a focus on the provision of increased support in schools, and unacceptable achievement gaps mean that educators experience schools that are changing from a one-size-fits-all format to one that involves more customization for students (CAST, 2018). Educators need models that support them to eradicate the achievement gap and provide differentiated support in caring classrooms that respond to both the academic and social-emotional needs of all students. The focus here is on three evidence-based practices that have been successful in supporting the educational needs of students and helping teachers to create classrooms where students can excel to include Differentiation of Instruction (Tomlinson, 2017), Creating Caring Classrooms (Ferguson et al., 2015), and Social and Emotional Skills and Learning (Taylor, Oberle, Durlak, & Weissberg, 2017).

Differentiation of Instruction

Students enter our school and classrooms with academic skills and strengths spread across a spectrum. There is a misperception that students leaving our schools should continue to be distributed across the same spectrum with roughly the same number of students receiving As and Fs, a few more students earning Bs and Ds, and the majority of students getting Cs, but it is that myth that perpetuates the achievement gap. School is an intervention and the goal should be for all students to master the material. Schools and teachers who truly desire to close the achievement gap must seek to completely destroy the normal curve and support all students to the point of achievement and mastery (Tomlinson, 2017).

When teachers deliver the same instruction to all students in the class, provide them with the same materials for learning, and assess learning in the same way, differentiation of instruction and learning has not occurred (Tomlinson, 2017). Some students will have done well; others will have done poorly; and instruction will continue irrespective of student outcome status. Simply put, instruction will be teacher-centered and, under this model, students who approach learning in different ways will not excel. When teachers customize instruction for each individual student in their class, they are not differentiating instruction; rather, they are trying to tailor instruction to what appear to be student needs and preferences in a subject area at a particular point in time. Teachers who individualize often find that they 'miss the mark' and are exhausted in their on-going efforts to support the diverse needs of each individual student in their class (Tomlinson, 2017).

Differentiation encourages teachers to meet students where they are; to become learner-centered; to teach to the needs of the students rather than to the components of a test; and to provide a menu of options for students so that they can select from that menu how they want to engage in learning (CAST, 2018). Teachers who differentiate do so in a variety of ways (Tomlinson, 2017). For example, they can:

- adjust the content that they teach by selecting a variety of materials that are germane to the task at hand, that are culturally relevant to students, and that peak their interest – all while responding to the standards that students must acquire;
- change the process of instruction to include small groups, peer learning, repeated short instructional cycles, and incorporate guided practice and brief formative assessments;
- adapt the products that students are asked to create to demonstrate their learning to incorporate music, videos, pictures, community performances, and, speech-to-text documents; and,
- change the affect/environment to include team learning, discussion, games, centers, and recognition that students have a choice.

Teachers who differentiate instruction well, know their students and provide instructional options that extend their learning journey, pique their interest, and are set at a level that meets their needs – a level at which students are ready to learn (CAST, 2018). Differentiation frees teachers to develop content, process, products and environments that engage students in a series of choices about their learning and how to demonstrate their classroom advances (Tomlinson, 2017). Differentiation can make instruction more fun for teachers and can make learning more fun for their students. This change in affect in a classroom can result in a change in how teachers view their job and in how students assess their teachers and their classroom experiences (Tomlinson, 2017). Students, from the earliest grades, can determine the extent to which their teachers care about them and their learning.

Creating Caring Classrooms

The Tripod Project was founded by Dr. Ronald Ferguson at Harvard University in the early 2000s (Ferguson & Danielson, 2014). The project engages a classroom level survey that sheds light on teaching practices and student engagement (Ferguson & Danielson, 2014). After a few decades of research with hundreds of thousands of students, analyses have generated seven key domains of teacher effectiveness (Tripod Education Partners, 2017). The seven teaching effectiveness domains are called the 7Cs. Student learning is better when effective teachers engage with instructional practices that incorporate these key domains (Tripod Education Partners, 2017).

- *Caring about students (nurturing productive relationships);*
- *Controlling behavior (promoting cooperation and peer support);*
- *Clarifying ideas and lessons (making success seem feasible);*
- *Challenging students to work hard and think hard (pressing for effort and rigor);*
- *Captivating students (making learning interesting and relevant);*
- *Conferring (eliciting students' feedback and respecting their ideas);*
- *Consolidating (connecting and integrating ideas to support learning).*

It is evident from Ferguson's work that children know the type of classroom environment in which they are sitting, and the type of classroom impacts their capacity to achieve (Ferguson & Danielson, 2014). The caring domain helps effective teachers to understand that students know when adults care about them (Ferguson et al., 2015). Effective teachers demonstrate that caring when they encourage students to talk to them; when they take the time to connect with students and pay attention to what they say, what they need, and what they do; when they remember information over time; and, when they select content or topics that are of interest to students. Controlling behavior helps students to feel safe. It helps students to predict what will happen. When students are encouraged to work in groups, cooperate, provide support to each other and essentially be team players, they can develop patterns of behavior that can help them to become productive and well-adjusted adults who have greater potential to retain a job (Ferguson et al., 2015). They have more agency over their own lives and can see a future.

Effective teachers clarify, challenge, and captivate students with their approach to instruction (Tripod Education Partners, 2017). Clarifying any misunderstandings for students, discussing ideas and approaches, and listening to their understanding of the requirements of a particular lesson can help them to produce work that is more '*on target*' and of higher quality (Ferguson & Danielson, 2014). Clarification can also calm a student's anxiety about the work, lead to greater focus on the task at hand, and help students to realize that they can be successful.

Challenges to work hard and think hard can increase achievement. Students can learn to exert effort, realize that hard work can reap rewards, and connect quality and hard work with success – especially when educators actively teach them to do so (Ferguson et al., 2015). Effective teachers know their students and present challenges that are manageable. They monitor student progress throughout a challenging situation and provide the support necessary for success. Captivating students and engaging them in quality learning opportunities that energize them is some of the most rewarding work an effective teacher can experience (Ferguson & Danielson, 2014). Captivating students engage in the magic that is teaching.

Effective teachers also confer and consolidate. Conferring with students means listening to them, hearing their ideas and what they say, and valuing their comments and ideas by adjusting what occurs in a classroom (when it's feasible to do so) – essentially letting them know that their contribution matters (Ferguson & Danielson, 2014). Consolidating is complex and involves all aspects of the classroom environment – instructional content, educator capacity, student needs, and how the various aspects interact and interconnect (Tripod Education Partners, 2017). Consolidating involves an on-going process of identifying, assessing, designing, implementing, evaluating, and monitoring and adjusting what's happening in a classroom - for everyone in the classroom (Ferguson et al., 2015). Consolidating can be a highly creative and unique process for all involved. Consolidating can move classrooms (and students) farther and faster when good/accurate connections are made, and learning can excel.

It may seem daunting to engage in all seven domains simultaneously. Perhaps begin with caring and controlling behavior to help to design an environment where it is conducive for all students to learn. Reviewing environmental adjustments through conferring and consolidating can help to refine what happens in the classroom and familiarize educators with their students – before moving to the review of the more academically focused domains of clarify, challenge, and captivate. Whichever process or sequence is selected, it is likely that educators not only become more effective in their instruction but also that they'll know more about their students and their social and emotional status and needs.

Social and Emotional Skills and Learning

To create a caring classroom, relationships are key. Students are more likely to have higher achievement when they feel connected to their school, teachers, and classmates (McNeely, Nonnemaker, & Blum, 2002). In order for students to feel connected, both they and their teachers must have the ability to manage their own emotions, behaviors and the skills to participate in healthy relationships. The Collaborative for Academic, Social, and Emotional Learning (CASEL, 2018) has consolidated research on social and emotional skills and condensed it into a *Framework for Systemic Social and Emotional Learning* containing five competencies:

- Self-Awareness: being able to label one's emotions, identify personal strengths, and build self-efficacy. Self-efficacy is a person's assessment of his or her own ability to perform within a domain. When students have high academic self-efficacy, they are more likely to persist even during difficult tasks. Self-efficacy can be built in four ways: 1) by having personal successes in the subject, 2) by seeing others like you have success at the task, 3) through the persuasion of friends and family, and 4) by connecting a positive emotional response, such as joy or pride, to a subject. Using differentiated instruction methods mentioned above, teachers are better able to create a learning environment that promotes self-efficacy.
- Self-Management: the strategies students use to regulate their emotions, stress levels, and impulsive behavior. These skills can be taught through teaching modeling and direct instruction. Giving students the tools necessary to manage their own behavior in the classroom is not only helpful in terms of overall classroom management, but can be very empowering to students whose learning differences either increase their hyperactivity and their anxiety
- Social-Awareness: Students with good social awareness are able to put themselves in another person's shoes. They can see and value multiple perspectives on a topic simultaneously. These students demonstrate respect and care for others.
- Relationship Skills: focus on the ability to engage with others in formal and informal settings. Not only are these skills key to a healthy, functioning classroom, but relationship skills and the ability to work with a diverse group of people are also sought after in the workplace.

- Responsible Decision-Making: The final competence of the CASEL model is Responsible Decision Making. This area synthesizes all of the other competencies and is defined as the "ability to make constructive choices about personal behavior and social interactions based on ethical standards, safety concerns, and social norms" (CASEL, 2018). Students with this competency should demonstrate prosocial classroom behaviors, academic honesty, and more positive studies habits.

When teachers model these skills and teach them through direct instruction to students, students are better equipped to deal with the social aspects of a diverse classroom and in turn feel more connected to their classmates and teachers.

Final Thoughts

America and its schools are changing. Effective teachers embrace this change and seek to meet every student where he or she is. Students come to school with unique strengths and challenges. Rather than seeing these differences as a hardship, educators must celebrate them as unique contributors to a rich learning environment. By combining differentiated instruction and social-emotional learning, educators can create caring classrooms that leverage students' strengths to close the achievement gap.

Points to Remember

- *Teachers must embrace the changes in education as the demographics and needs of students change.*
- *Teachers must not only know their academic content (the what of teaching) and how to teach (the how of teaching) but must know their students and their unique needs (the who they are teaching).*
- *Differentiated instruction is a sustainable way to reach students of differing ability levels.*
- *Teachers that create caring classroom environments help students to feel safe and secure during the learning process.*
- *Teaching students social and emotional skills helps students to actively participate in the social environment and to manage their own learning behaviors.*

References

Association of Teacher Education. (2018). *Standards for teacher educators*. Retrieved from https://www.ate1.org/standards-for-teacher-educators.

Auhl, G. & Daniel, G.R. (2014). Preparing pre-service teachers for the profession: Creating spaces for transformative practice. *Journal of Education for Teaching, 40*(4), 377-390. DOI: 10.1080/02607476.2014.924649

CAST. (2018). *About universal design for learning*. Retrieved from http://www.cast.org/our-work/about-udl.html#.W_tgzOhKg2w

Collaborative for Academic, Social, and Emotional Learning [CASEL]. (2018). What is SEL?, retrieved from https://casel.org/what-is-sel/.

Copeland, W. E., Keeler, G., Angold, A., & Costello, E. J. (2007). Traumatic events and posttraumatic stress in childhood. *Archives of General Psychiatry, 64*(5), 577-584. doi:10.1001/archpsyc.64.5.577

Darling-Hammond, L. (2006). Constructing 21st-century teacher education. *Journal of teacher education, 57*(3), 300-314. doi:10.1177/0022487105285962

Durlak, J. A., Weissberg, R. P., Dymnicki, A. B., Taylor, R. D., & Schellinger, K. B. (2011). The impact of enhancing students' social and emotional learning: A meta-analysis of school-based universal interventions. *Child Development, 82*(1), 405-432. doi:10.1111/j.14678624.2010.01564.x

Ferguson, R. F., & Danielson, C. (2014). How framework for teaching and tripod 7Cs evidence distinguish key components of effective teaching. In T. J. Kane, K. A. Kerr, & R. C. Pianta (Eds.), *Designing teacher evaluation systems: New guidance from the measures of effective teaching project* (pp. 98–143). San Francisco, CA: Jossey-Bass.

Ferguson, R. F., Phillips, S. F., Rowley, J. F., & Friedlander, J. W. (2015). *The influence of teaching beyond standardized test scores: Engagement, mindsets, and agency*. Cambridge, MA: Achievement Gap Initiative, Harvard University. Retrieved from http://www.agi.harvard.edu/projects/TeachingandAgency.pdf.

Gay, G. (2005). *A synthesis of scholarship in multicultural education*. Naperville, IL: North Central Regional Educational Laboratory.

Hansen, M., Levesque, E.M., Quintero, D., & Valant, J. *Have we made progress on achievement gaps? Looking at evidence from the new NAEP results*. Retrieved from https://www.brookings.edu/blog/brown-center-chalkboard/2018/04/17/have-we-made-progress-on-achievement-gaps-looking-at-evidence-from-the-new-naep-results/

Ladson-Billings, G. (1995). Toward a theory of culturally relevant pedagogy. *American Educational Research Journal, 32*(3), 465-491. doi: 10.3102/00028312032003465

McFarland, J., Hussar, B., Wang, X., Zhang, J., Wang, K., Rathbun, A., ... & Bullock Mann, F. (2018). *The condition of education 2018* (NCES 2018-144). Washington, DC: U.S. Department of Education, National Center for Education Statistics. Retrieved from https://nces.ed.gov/pubsearch/pubsinfo.asp?pubid=2018144.

McNeely, C. A., Nonnemaker, J. M., & Blum, R. W. (2002). Promoting school connectedness: Evidence from the national longitudinal study of adolescent health. *Journal of School Health, 72*(4), 137- 146. doi:10.1111/j.1746-1561.2002.tb06533.x

Merriam, S. B., & Bierema, L. L. (2014). *Adult learning: Linking theory and practice.* San Francisco, CA: Jossey-Bass.

Musu-Gillette, L., de Brey, C., McFarland, J., Hussar, W., Sonnenberg, W., & Wilkinson-Flicker, S. (2017). *Status and trends in the education of racial and ethnic groups 2017* (NCES 2017-051). Washington, DC: U.S. Department of Education, National Center for Education Statistics. Retrieved from https://nces.ed.gov/pubsearch/pubsinfo.asp?pubid=2017051.

Planty, M., Hussar, W., Snyder, T., Provasnik, S., Kena, G., Dinkes, R., Kewal Ramani, A., & Kemp, J. (2008). The Condition of Education 2008 (NCES 2008-031). National Center for Education Statistics, Institute of Education Sciences, U.S. Department of Education. Washington, DC.

Snyder, T.D. De Brey, C. & Dillow, S.A. (2018). Digest of Education Statistics 2016 (NCES 2017-094. National Center for Education Statistics, Institute of Education Sciences, U.S. Department of Education, Washing Ton, DC., 2017

Taylor, R. D., Oberle, E., Durlak, J. A., & Weissberg, R. P. (2017). Promoting positive youth development through school-based social and emotional learning interventions: A meta-analysis of follow-up effects. *Child Development, 88*(4), 1156-1171. doi:10.1111/cdev.12864

Tomlinson, C. A. (2017). How to differentiate instruction in academically diverse classrooms (3rd ed.). Alexandria, VA: ASCD.

Tomlinson, C., & Doubet, K. (2005). Reach them to teach them. *Educational Leadership, 62*(7), 8-15.

Torraco, R. (2018). Economic inequality, educational inequality, and reduced career opportunity: A self-perpetuating cycle? *New Horizons in Adult Education and Human Resource Development, 30*(1). DOI: 10.1002/nha3.20206

Tripod Education Partners. (2017). *Guide to Tripod's 7Cs framework.* Retrieved from https://tripoded.com/teacher-toolkit/

Well, A.S., Fox, L., & Cordova-Cobo, D. (2016). *How racially diverse schools and classrooms can benefit all students.* Retrieved from https://tcf.org/content/report/how-racially-diverse-schools-and-classrooms-can-benefit-all-students/?session=1

Young, N.D., Jean (Bienia), E. & Citro, T.A. (2018a). *From head to heart: High quality Teaching practices in the spotlight.* Wilmington, DE: Vernon Press.

Young, N.D., Jean (Bienia), E. & Citro, T.A. (2018b). *Stars in the schoolhouse: Teaching practices and approaches that make a difference.* Wilmington, DE: Vernon Press.

Young, N.D., Jean (Bienia), E. & Mead, A.E. (2018). *The potency of the principalship: Action-oriented leadership to support student achievement.* Wilmington, DE: Vernon Press.

Chapter Seven

Social Justice Curricula: Design and Implementation Across the Content Areas

Nicholas D. Young, *American International College*

Ashley Adamski, *American International College*

Social justice has been defined in a number of ways throughout the decades and regardless of the theory, it is often described not as what social justice is, but what it is not; the injustices of oppression, prejudice, and racism (Wade, 2007). Social justice can be defined, broadly, as a perspective that everyone warrants the same economic, political and social rights and equalities; regardless of race, socioeconomic status, gender or other characteristics (Adams & Bell, 2016). This definition is intentionally broad as social justice encompasses both historical and critical examinations of justice issues (Capeheart & Milovanovic, 2007). It is also important to note that social justice and the interpretation of the definition may vary by individuals based on personal and professional experiences of working with the definition. While there are some variations in the definition, which in turn could vary curricula for classrooms, the teachers within a district should come to a general understanding and working definition that supports positive change (Harmon, 2015). Unity in the definition will allow for scaffolding to occur on the topic as students move through different grade levels, with the ability to build on topics and activities that were discussed in earlier social justice classes (Harmon, 2015). Social justice also has workings in both historical and current events. The historical and current elements of social justice can be integrated into the curricula developed within the classroom, as both are essential for understanding the dynamics of the topic and ways to promote social equity (Adams & Bell, 2016).

The need for courses related to social justice and human rights has risen as there has been more of a focus on the injustices of society and ways that non-dominant characteristics are discriminated against (Adams & Bell, 2016). Educators are able to introduce and teach the topic of social justice in the classroom as the majority of students in the United States spend just less than 1,000 hours in school each year (Bush, Ryan, & Rose, 2011; Hull & Newport, 2011). The large amount of time spent in classrooms can be used to educate and influence positive social change, especially when the information is presented in a way that inspires and interests the students (Armstrong, 2016). Some texts emphasize that social justice has become a 'buzzword' in society that can relate to a wide range of practices and values, at times losing focus on the primary goals; therefore, social justice curricula should have a direct focus on the issues that are truly relevant and strive towards positive change and social equity (Agarwal-Rangnath, 2013).

Creating a social justice curriculum requires creativity, understanding, and compassion on the part of the teacher, as there are limited clear-cut requirements for the topic. Teachers should be familiar with the definition of social justice and social equity when developing a course. This can be done through the reading of social justice texts, trainings during or after their graduate training, or mentorship with a seasoned social justice educator (Blake, 2015; Kaur, 2012). The scholarship of social justice should examine what justice means and how this is viewed and/or implemented in a variety of social contexts (Capeheart & Milovanovic, 2007). A deep understanding of social justice as a concept and way of living is necessary in order to teach or develop curricula for the classroom; thus, the focus of the curricula will focus on the primary goals of social justice, while promoting changes towards social equity (Wade, 2007). Teachers with a better understanding of the concept will be able to develop a strong curriculum as well as promote inspiration within their students. When a concept is better understood, the manner in which it is taught is more fluid and natural; allowing for strong and thoughtful discussions to occur in the classroom.

Social justice has become a focal point of learning in the K-12 classrooms, with teachers challenging students to examine the world around them and make changes within themselves and their community (Agarwal-Rangnath, 2013). Well-structured curriculums help to shape the way that academic material is delivered and taught to the students (National Education Association, 2017). Traditional curriculums have failed to serve students outside of the mainstream demographics. Recently improved social justice curricula help to combat the historical inequalities of traditional curricula and learning that comes from a dominant culture (Agarwal et al., 2010; National Education Association, 2017). While there are influences from the administration and educational boards, teachers have some flexibility in how and what is taught in their classrooms; therefore, teachers should consider what material should be included when preparing for a social justice class or developing a curriculum. Curricula can vary between classrooms and individual styles of the teacher; yet, the goals for a social justice class should remain consistent.

The goals of social justice education should be on awareness, promotion of individual and community change, and movement towards social equity (Hackman, 2006). The focus of the social justice classroom may also vary based on the academic grade that is being taught with themes and objectives expanding as the academic grades progress; thus, teachers of kindergarten through fifth grade classrooms will develop a foundation of learning social justice issues that can be expanded as the student moves through middle and high school (Dell'Angelo, 2014). More attention would be put on the promotion of change and activism at the high school level.

Curricula should be focused on culturally relevant and equity-orientated instruction that helps to close and address the achievement gap (Dorman, 2012). The teachers may create this curriculum from a foundation of being diversity-prepared, with education on how to appropriately address these sensitive issues within a diverse student classroom (Adams & Bell, 2016; Dell'Angelo, 2014). All grade levels should have curricula that addresses diversity within the classroom and is created from a place of equality and understanding. The topics in a social justice curriculum may be sensitive to students that are experiencing the issues addressed and, therefore, should be taught in a manner that does not bring further prejudice or biases. The curriculum should be both culturally relevant and responsive, with these two concepts helping to build classroom communities with dialogues that include differences (Agarwal et al., 2010).

Agarwal-Rangnath, 2013, discusses five tenets that should be included in all social justice curricula to include inspiring wonder, painting the picture, application of skills, connecting the past to the present, and facilitating change (Agarwal-Rangnath, 2013; Agarwal-Rangnath et al., 2016). These five tenets help to support the development of the curricula and can apply to any educational or grade level. Earlier grade levels may focus more on the inspiration and painting a picture aspects of the tenet, as this may be viewed as a more foundational or beginning piece; however, there are ways to facilitate change even in the earlier elementary grades (Agarwal-Rangnath, 2013).

Social Justice Curricula in the K-5 Classroom

Teachers can begin to build an understanding of social justice at an early age with students. A national Gallup student poll found that 75% of elementary school students were interested and actively involved in their school classrooms (Armstrong, 2016). This large percent shows that students are interested and willing to learn; making elementary school the ideal period to begin with foundational and inspiration for change through social justice curricula (Armstrong, 2016). Social justice issues are relevant to children of elementary school age where many are struggling with issues such as poverty, hunger, and racism (White, Hill, Kemp, MacRae, & Young, 2012). Identifying and understanding these issues in the classroom setting may elicit feelings that promote learning more about the injustices and ways to promote social equity (White et al., 2016). Children carry knowledge and expertise about their own lives that can be used to engage in meaningful participation in social activism projects (Torres-Harding, Baber, Hilvers, Hobbs, & Maly, 2018). Teachers can individualize the social justice curriculum that they develop to adhere to the demographics of the school district and what they feel would be important to the students in their classroom; however, all issues of social justice are important to include as a national and worldwide view of issues helps to understand the greater problems of injustice (Agarwal-Rangnath et al., 2016)

The curriculum for social justice in the elementary setting should have a focus on the foundational issues (Dell'Angelo, 2014). During the early elementary grades, the curriculum can also focus on ethnic identity to help students become culturally sensitive to their own identities and those of others in the classroom and in the greater community (Dell'Angelo, 2014). Studies have shown that youth engagement in social activism programs within the classroom may help students to develop improved self-efficacy and positive cultural identity (Torres-Harding et al., 2018). Elementary social justice curricula can help to enhance self-love and respect for others. Teachers can promote these concepts in the students by providing opportunities to learn where they, and others, come from. This can help to deconstruct negative stereotypes about different cultural and ethnic identities and allows for respect for others when students share their different stories and knowledge about their own cultural backgrounds (Picower, 2012). This is easily added to the curriculum by creating projects in which students interview their family members to gather an understanding about their backgrounds and then share with the rest of the class. This foundational activity allows for identification to occur in a positive manner and understand the potential diversity of other students in the classroom. This can continue to be built upon in future grades; thus, establishing social understanding and empathy allows for scaffolding on social justice issues.

Curricula for the Middle School Classroom

Middle school can vary in ages and grades depending on the state and school district; however, for the purposes of this text, the definition of middle school refers to students within the sixth through eighth grade. This is a period of change and possible turbulence for students as they move through adolescence (Armstrong, 2016). The period of adolescence has been described by psychologist Erik Erikson as a time where there is a struggle between two forces, one force that seeks an identity in the world and the other that creates a role of confusion (Armstrong, 2016). Social justice curricula vary from elementary school to middle school as the older students are more mature and prefer more frequent opportunities to make their own choices regarding what they learn and are interested in learning (Armstrong, 2016). This allows for the educator to establish a curriculum that allows for flexibility and input from the students. The educator may find more active participation when the students are allowed to discuss issues that are relevant to them, but that also fit in with the requirements of the social justice curricula. Educators may ask students to do at home projects where they look for articles, both locally and nationally, that relate to the topic at certain points in the curricula (National Education Association, 2017). The curricula will also vary at this educational level as the continuum will continue as the high schools will go more in depth and have greater opportunities for the students to participate in social justice activities outside of the classroom. With the understanding that change and identity seeking during the middle school time period occurs in great proportions, teachers for grades six through eight may want to center their social justice curricula around different identities (National Education Association, 2017). The topics could introduce the different identities in society, both dominant and non-dominant, and help to provide understanding and promote equity. Middle school students may be more interested in their dynamic of social justice learning and feel empowered to make positive changes to the identity that they are coming into. Social justice curricula with a focus on identity development at the middle school grade level may promote a more positive community environment in the school, with a greater understanding towards diverse identity developments (National Education Association, 2017).

Knowledge of social justice can be developed through a number of activities that can provide an initial understanding of social justice. One study looked at the addition of grassroots campaigns, or GRCs, to school curriculums (Torres-Harding et al., 2018). A qualitative analysis of the GRC in classrooms showed that students responded positively to this and developed knowledge of inequality, how the social problems affected their communities, and what change was needed (Torres-Harding et al., 2018). The GRCs are collaborative and student-centered and completed in the classroom where a problem has been identified and a multicultural perspective is used to analyze the problems (Torres-Harding et al., 2018). The problem identified will be chosen by the classroom, and there may be several possible problems that are discussed before one is collaboratively chosen. Once the problem is chosen the students work to identify the causes of the problem, including why the problem started and how it affects the community (Torres-Harding et al., 2018). The students will look at information and possibly participate in outreach activities to connect with groups or individuals in the community regarding the issue. Through the research and interviews conducted, the students develop goals and action plans to initiate positive change. During the entire process, students participate in a cycle of reflection, individually and as a group, on their experiences and what the next steps for action might include (Torres-Harding et al., 2018).

During middle school, there can be a chance for out of school opportunities, yet this requires educator supervision. Teachers in certain school districts may find this to be challenging as they are not able to take students outside of the classroom or on school trips as frequently as other districts; however, the social justice educator should take the students out of the classroom when possible to places such as local museums or service-learning experiences (Harmon, 2015; Maayan, 2018). Since it may be difficult to have these done during school times, service-learning experiences could be incorporated as an after-school approach for either extra credit or part of the curricula in a project setting (Carnicelli & Boluk, 2017). Service learning helps to tie in classroom academics to practical application by students offering services to their communities and has been shown to enhance students' sense of social responsibility and can promote social justice understanding through reduction of stereotypes and understanding different social groups (Carnicelli & Boluk, 2017; Zimmerman, Krachick, & Aberle, 2009). Students at the middle school level may be responsive to this as they would be able to choose which social cause they would like to participate in; thus, these students would also bring diversity to classroom discussions regarding personal service learning experiences.

Social Justice in the High School Classroom

High school is a time where promotion of change and ideas for change can be facilitated. Students are at the time where they will be completing their secondary education and moving on to employment or higher education opportunities; therefore, high school is a time where the social justice curricula must have connections to the life-paths that will be taken after graduation (National Education Association, 2017). Wade (2007) has described social justice as a process of working toward meeting everyone's basic needs and fulfilling the potential to live productively. High school social justice classes would naturally have this focus as individuals are moving towards productive and fulfilling lives after graduation. The curriculum is developed to scaffold opportunities for students to be active participants in their community for civic engagement and change (Agarwal et al., 2010). Students at the high school level have matured enough throughout their school career and life experiences to understand the connections that are made (Osler, 2016). Students can relate to the philosophy of wanting to live their most productive and fulfilling lives, while acknowledging a variety of boundaries within the social structure and society that could hinder or prevent this (Hollenbach, (2017).

Curricula for high school will have the most in-depth focus into social justice, as with age and experience many students are able to be exposed to different areas of social justice and relate this back to their own personal experiences and those occurring within current events (Osler, 2016). During these grade levels, teachers are able to challenge students to examine the world around them and to make positive changes within their communities (Agarwal-Rangnath, 2013, Agarwal-Rangnath, Dover, & Henning, 2016). Teachers may wish to express that small, positive changes can help to facilitate social justice which, in turn, will help students apply the teachings of the class to larger activities within the school and communities (Osler, 2016). The teacher, for example, may encourage more acceptance towards diversity in both the school and with peers. The curriculum may discuss issues that are relevant to the city where the school is located or the issues of diversity within the student body (National Education Association, 2017). The foundational understanding and empathy that was developed in elementary school will be used to create an environment of sensitivity when discussing the injustices of social issues (Harmon, 2015). The educator should use a multicultural and non-dominant perspective on the issues, while showing students how the dominant perspective and culture has facilitated the inequality (Osler, 2016).

Textbooks are often required materials for classroom education; however, a supplement to the textbook would be at least one of the many novels written about or in regard to social justice. An internet search will bring about a number of novels written from the perspectives of those that have been oppressed (Bassett, Bigham, & Calvert, 2017). New and current issues; including sexual oppression and sexual harassment may require that material outside of the traditional textbook be used. For high school students, reading a book that is written as a firsthand account may connect them more to the material and help identify (Bassett et al., 2017). Some textbooks do not create the narrative where the student can feel and live in the oppressive state, and fully understand the emotions and dynamics involved; therefore, the educator should discuss the material in class and engage the students to think more critically about it as a problem larger than the individual affected.

Another educational supplement, especially for the high school level classroom, would be to use global, national, and local issues (Spiegler, 2016). The curriculum should allow for flexibility to include current events. The educator can tie in current events; for example, when students or staff bring in news articles to have a deeper and more unique perspective of the topics discussed. The students may become more aware of the number of social justice issues that are happening nationally and locally. There can also be connections to how these current events have roots in past social justice issues; adding more understanding that some issues in social justice history can occur repeatedly (Spiegler, 2016). Using current events allows for a broader and more individualized classroom curriculum. Teaching directly from the textbook, without the encouragement of critical thinking about the subject, may negate the experiences discussed in the text, or not present the issues in a way that allows understanding for the greater social justice problem, and does not allow for the educator to look at the diverse issues of his or her own classroom and create a curriculum that is based on the students and their community (Agarwal-Rangnath et al., 2016). Social justice issues have been shown to inspire change, especially when the individual feels a personal connection to the issue discussed (Agarwal-Rangnath, 2013). Student involvement in the curriculum and classroom discussion can help to lead to richer and deeper conversations and understanding of the social justice issues.

Final Thoughts

Social justice issues are important to teach at all grade levels of the K-12 classroom. Educators would benefit from having meetings within their schools or districts that would allow for scaffolding to occur as a social justice curriculum is developed throughout the levels. This would ensure students could move from a foundational understanding of social justice at the elementary grades to more inspired levels of activism at the high school level. Social justice curricula should be flexible and not rely solely on a textbook as some of the best examples are real-world current happenings. Educators and students should use current events or issues within their community to drive classroom discussions and elicit motivations for positive change. Educators should create curricula with a multicultural and non-dominant perspective.

Points to Remember

- *Social justice curricula should inspire, educate, and facilitate change inside and outside the classroom communities.*
- *Teachers should address material in a culturally responsive and culturally sensitive manner to help students learn the concepts in a way that encourages differences and diversity.*
- *Social justice curricula can be created at all grade levels, with elementary school students learning foundational components of social justice and having this material expanded upon throughout the academic years.*
- *Teachers should bring in current events and personal experiences as well as encourage students to do the same, to help inspire change and have students motivated to be more active in social justice change and education.*
- *Materials other than textbooks should be used with outside school activities, such as service-learning experiences being included in the curriculum. Effective social justice curricula break the standard and teach from a multicultural perspective, especially from groups that are marginalized.*

References

Adams, M. & Bell, L.A. (2016). *Teaching for diversity and social justice* (3rd ed.). New York, NY: Routledge

Agarwal-Rangnath, R. (2013). *Social Studies, Literacy, and Social Justice in the Common Core Classroom: A Guide for Teachers.* New York, NY: Teachers College Press.

Agarwal-Rangnath, R., Dover, A.G., & Henning, N. (2016). *Preparing to teach social studies for social justice: Becoming a renegade.* New York, NY: Teachers College, Columbia University

Armstrong, T. (2016). *The Power of the Adolescent Brain: Strategies for Teaching Middle and High School Students.* Alexandria, VA: ASCD.

Bassett, K., Bigham, B., & Calvert, L. (eds.). (2017). *Social justice book list.* Retrieved from https://www.nnstoy.org/wp-content/uploads/2017/08/NNSTOY-Social-Justice-Book-List.pdf

Blake, C. (2015). *Teaching social justice in theory and practice.* Retrieved from https://education.cu-portland.edu/blog/classroom-resources/teaching-social-justice/

Bush, M., Ryan, M., & Rose, S. (2011). *School calendar: Number of instructional days/hours in the school year.* Retrieved from http://www.ecs.org/clearinghouse/95/05/9505.pdf

Capeheart, L. & Milovanovic, D. (2007). *Social Justice: Theories, Issues, and Movements.* Piscataway, NJ: Rutgers University Press.

Carnicelli, S. & Boluk, K. (2017). The promotion of social justice: Service learning for transformative education. *Journal of hospitality, leisure, sport & tourism education, 21*(B), 126-134. DOI: 10.1016/j.jhlste.2017.01.003

Dell'Angelo, T. (2014). *Creating classrooms for social justice.* Retrieved from https://www.edutopia.org/blog/creating-classrooms-for-social-justice-tabitha-dellangelo

Dorman, E.H. (2012). Teaching for social justice and equity in small urban high schools: Challenges and possibilities. *Online Yearbook of Urban Learning: Teaching and Research,* 1-14. Retrieved from https://files.eric.ed.gov/fulltext/EJ980016.pdf

Hackman, H.W. (2006). Five essential components for social justice education. *Equity & Excellence in Education, 38*(2), 103-109. DOI: 10.1080/10665680590935034

Harmon, J. (2015). *Social justice: A whole-school approach.* Retrieved from https://www.edutopia.org/blog/social-justice-whole-school-approach-jeanine-harmon

Hull, J. & Newport, M. (2011). Time in school: How does the U.S. compare? *Center for Public Education.* Retrieved from http://www.centerforpubliceducation.org/research/time-school-how-does-us-compare

Kaur, B. (2012). Equity and social justice in teaching and teacher education. *Teaching and Teacher Education, 28,* 485-482. DOI: 10.1016/j.tate.2012.01.012

Maayan, C. (2018). *Middle school social justice trips bring meaning to young teens.* Retrieved from https://prizmah.org/middle-school-social-justice-trips-bring-meaning-young-teens

National Education Association. (2017). *Social justice lesson plans.* Retrieved from http://www.nea.org/grants/63178.htm

Osler, A. (2016). *Human Rights and Schooling: An ethical framework for teaching social justice.* New York, NJ: Teachers College, Columbia University

Picower, B. (2012). Using their words: Six elements of social justice curriculum design for the elementary classroom. *International Journal of Multicultural Education, 14*(1), 1-17. DOI: 10/18251/ijme.v14i1.484

Spiegler, J. (2016). *Turning current events instruction into social justice teaching.* Retrieved from https://www.edutopia.org/blog/current-events-social-justice-teaching-jinnie-spiegler

Torres-Harding, S. Baber, A., Hilvers, J., Hobbs, N., & Maly, M. (2018). Children as agents of social and community change: Enhancing youth empowerment through participation in a school-based social activism project. *Education, Citizenship, and Social Justice, 13*(1), 3-18. DOI: 10.1177/1746197916684643

Wade, R.C. (2007). *Social studies for social justice: Teaching strategies for the elementary classroom,* New York, NY: Teachers College

White, M., Hill, I., Kemp, S., MacRae, J., & Young, L. (2016). *Poverty and education survey: A teacher's perspective: Staff awareness and understanding about poverty issues.* Retrieved from https://bctf.ca/uploadedFiles/Public/SocialJustice/Issues/Poverty/Research/BCTF%20Poverty%20and%20Education--Chapter%206.pdf

Zimmerman, T.S., Krachick, J.L., & Aberle, J.T. (2009). A university service-learning assignment: Delivering the FAIR curriculum to K-12 students to promote social justice. *Education, Citizenship, and Social Justice, 4*(3), 195-210. DOI: 10.1177/1746197909340875

Chapter Eight

Student Leadership: A Necessary Component in Equity Education

Nicholas D. Young, *American International College*

Aimee Dalenta, *Goodwin College*

Social standards and norms are shifting in today's modern society, and the field of education is developing and changing, modifying and growing, alongside the oftentimes shaky landscape that surrounds it. As social movements are cultivated, the best educational leaders have heard the calls for fairness and equal treatment throughout a vast range of educational settings (Masters, 2018). Issues of equity in education have been called to the forefront of our collective consciousness. No longer can society as a whole brush aside issues that perpetuate the educational divide, such as unequal funding and unfair access to learning opportunities. Gone are the days of accepting racial, gender, and ability biases. Overthrowing the complacency is a robust rising of voices speaking out on behalf of marginalized populations. Now, communities are being asked to face the difficult truths about equity in education; these truths are divisive, and oftentimes painful (Gonzales & Weiner, 2017). These truths raise more questions than they do answers. Nonetheless, they are truths that must be addressed to make way for a more equitable educational future for all children living in this country. With increased tension and an unclear picture of the role of the stability of educational leadership on a national level, equity education is on the forefront of writing a new chapter for 21st century education.

Though equity and equality are terms often used interchangeably, the two have several distinct features (Masters, 2018). Equity approaches inequalities as an opportunity to compensate those left marginalized. The aim of equity education is to level the proverbial playing field; equity education strives to provide more support to those who need it most, rather than provide all students with the exact same thing. The goal of equity education is to assure that all students have access to the same quality education, even if there is ultimately unequal distribution of services (Masters, 2018). Students in a low income, underperforming district, for example, may need access to different or more expensive programs to raise reading scores. Students in a middle-income district may already have adequate reading scores and, therefore, would not need the additional reading program; thus, the foundation of equity education emerges: the goal of helping students reach a proficient reading level is attained in both school districts, but one district receives extra resources. It is fair, however, it is not equal.

In 2017, researchers from Yale conducted a study that examined the way people understood equality. Interestingly, the results suggest that, in general, individuals value fairness over equivalence (Stamans, Sheskin, & Bloom, 2017). In several psychological experiments, children as young as six display a strong aversion to inequality and, overall, evidence suggests that adults also show a positive bias for distributing resources based on merit or need (Masters, 2018). Based on the findings in this study, it can be assumed that the majority of individuals studied would believe in the value system behind the concept of equity education.

Equity education can also pertain to those individuals who have exceptional learning needs (Cruz & Stake, 2012). These individuals may require a different learning facility, additional staff members, or other learning supports in order to create a successful learning environment unique to their needs. These supports require more money and resources, requiring districts to allocate large sums of money to students in special education programs (Walker, 2013). Students in general education classrooms cost a district significantly less per pupil. At play in this scenario is the fundamental approach to equity education, where all students are given access to resources that they need to be successful, regardless if others receive the same thing.

The concept of equity education has fully emerged after generations of a deeply divided educational system in the United States. Defined as "each child receiving what he or she needs to develop to his or her fully academic and social potential," (National Equity Project, 2017, n.p.) equity gives each student what he or she needs to be successful. It does not give every student the exact same thing. As federal education laws have evolved over time, so has the nation's demographics, both racially and otherwise. Recent estimates suggest that the majority of public school students are students of color, and that 20% of school-aged children are living in poverty (Musu-Gillette, de Brey, McFarland, Hussar, Sonnenberg, & Wilkinson-Flicker, (2017). Furthermore, it is estimated that 15% of all students in public education ages 3-18 receive special education services (Taylor, Smily, & Richards, 2015). Exploring this data further reveals that the percentage of students in leadership positions do not mirror the demographics (Taylor et al., 2015). In this modern era, it is critical that students and young people see their peer leaders as representative of themselves, both in race, gender, and beyond.

To create a scenario of equity in an educational setting, the role of the student leader is paramount (Haber-Curran & Tilapaugh, 2017). Student leaders set the tone for the culture at a school or within a district. Student leaders are often the face of a student group at large and become an official or unofficial spokesperson representing many of their peers. It cannot be overlooked that, too often, leaders emerge in a group based on biases and privileges (Haber-Curran & Zulpizio, 2017). To create more equity, all students regardless of academic or economical need should be considered and encouraged to embrace leadership roles.

Student leadership is not a stagnant role; rather it is a state of mind and a state of being. Leadership is a quality that can be taught and cultivated; one is not simply born with attributes of an effective leader; thus, "leadership is learnable-it begins with leading oneself" (Bowen, 2014). It is increasingly important, therefore, that leadership skills be explicitly taught beginning at a young age, especially in the most high-needs schools or to the most high-needs students. Like any other academic skill, leadership consists of teachable components and a vast array of opportunity; however, districts must be willing to support programs that sustain student leadership initiatives (Bowen, 2014). By empowering students in all schools and districts, educators are helping to prepare them for lifetimes of advocacy, equality, and success.

Student leaders are a necessary element in a school's ecosystem. While student leaders are imperative in all academic settings as a representative voice, active and engaged student leaders are especially critical in more marginalized school districts, and must represent the races, ethnicities, genders, and cognitive abilities of the student population as a whole (Haber-Curran & Tillapaugh, 2017). Students leaders should speak for the voice of the collective student population. Leaders are empowered to stand up for social changes from within the school, advocate for fairness, and think broadly about actionable change. Many times, leaders emerge through necessity and natural inclination (Myers, 2018). Most often, research suggests that potential leaders need to be given the opportunity to embrace this role, and the support to grow into it (Myers, 2018). As a nation, the backdrop of equity education will continue to elevate students of all races, creeds, ability levels, and genders into successful leadership roles (Aspen Institute, 2018). It is the duty of school administrators, community leaders, and other school officials to understand the implications of equitable student leadership on the population of students as a whole (Rimmer, n.d.).

Components and Strategies for Cultivating Leadership

There are many accepted definitions of the term 'leadership skills.' Doyle (2018) suggests that there are five essential leadership skills necessary to include communication, creativity, feedback, motivation, and positivity. These skills, all in conjunction with one another, can foster an environment where individuals are developing characteristics that inspire and transform both themselves and others. Hine (2014) presented five contemporary models of leadership to inlcude transactional, transformational, charismatic, servant, and distributed leadership. Based on personality types and leadership development programs, individuals usually have more than one avenue to pursue in regards to the skill set they develop as leaders.

Students should be given tangible goals to reach for leadership development. Some of these goals may include focusing on daily habits and progress, redefining failure, and bolstering reflection techniques (Clark, 2017; Elmore, 2017). These, along with other support techniques, can help a student build leadership skills necessary for a successful foundation. In equity education, it is critical that teachers and school leaders take seriously the job of offering these skills to all students, especially those students from marginalized populations (Rimmer, n.d.). These students have just as much potential to develop leadership skills as other students, yet they often need to be explicitly given the opportunity to do so.

In one recent study, experts examined leadership development and the importance of the family unit in fostering a child's leadership skills (Balikci, 2018). The attitudes, behaviors, and education level of parents play a crucial role in this very development (Balikci, 2018). Mothers who were more highly educated and more involved in their child's academics produced students who were more likely to ascend to leadership positions. Students in leadership positions were more likely to come from families in financially secure situations, as well as families who were able to financially support extracurricular interests (Balikci, 2018). This study reveals an unfortunate and enormous gap in student leadership representation and indicates that there is much work to be done to continue to improve the situation (Balikci, 2018).

There is evidence of a strong connection and respect between teacher and student that leads to better student outcomes and this is also true as it pertains to student leadership development (Blazar & Kraft, 2017). When students have a trusted adult in their educational community that encourages their leadership development, they are more likely to successfully cultivate the qualities of a leader (Blazar & Kraft, 2017). Students who are encouraged to seek leadership roles, and who are provided with opportunities to embark on collaborative learning experiences are better able to develop their growth mindset. Young people should be encouraged to develop their sense of self-acceptance, lower their need for perfectionism, and focus on the eminent improvements they can make on a personal journey, which in turn helps develop leadership skills (United Nations Educational, Scientific, and Cultural Organization, 2017). Positive interactions between students and teachers or administrators correlate with effective development of a student leader (Balikci, 2018). When teachers show personal interest in a student, and students feel a positive connection to the teacher, they are more likely to pursue leadership opportunities within the school. These students feel supported and championed, which raises confidence and self-efficacy.

Developing Student Leadership Through Service Learning

Conventional wisdom of the past indicates that leadership was a natural, innate state of being that lucky and fortunate individuals were simply born with (Winch, 2015). When leaders arose on a small or large scale, it was believed that they were simply more adept and had more natural ability to influence people. Modern research simply proves this outdated theory wrong: individuals can acquire skills that hone, develop, and improve their leadership abilities (Winch, 2015). Individuals can progress their listening skills, sense of ethics, collaborative skills, and more through explicit training that begins at a young age. One such activity that imparts leadership qualities in young people is to expose them to service learning projects.

Integrated into the academic curriculum, service learning projects bring civic life into full view, allowing students time to improve the community they live in, while later reflecting on their role (Carnicelli, & Boluk, 2017). In equity education, this structure has immense potential. Students can choose activities that speak to their interests and passions. Students can explicitly choose service learning projects that better their community and help to level the playing field—the primary goal of equity education itself (Carnicelli, & Boluk, 2017).

Service learning projects improve confidence and knowledge among student leaders (Carnicelli, & Boluk, 2017). Students who participate in service-learning projects report being ready for more responsibilities in school, including peer mentoring and other such leadership roles (Carnicelli, & Boluk, 2017). Empowering students increases their involvement with their school and community as a whole, which could help with career choices and, ultimately, give students an advantage in the job market (Lund, 2018). This type of project has clear positive implications for more marginalized students, as it encourages and applauds individuals for joining in efforts to improve the community at large (Lund, 2018).

Strategies for Leadership Development

Mirroring so many critical components of character development and team building initiatives, learning positive communication skills is vital to leadership development. Understanding how to connect and empathize with individuals in the community will help build trust between leaders and their constituents, as well as help build a well-rounded and supportive leader within a community (Blazar & Kraft, 2017). In turn, this skill set will also benefit the student leader in a school setting, allowing him or her to practice and develop important communication skills. In a school, a student leader must see examples of teachers demonstrating these communication skills such as listening, empathizing, and problem solving with others (Black, Walsh, Magee, Hutchins, Berman, & Groundwater-Smith, 2014). When adults have a clear understanding of their leadership skills, they are better able to support their students' leadership development (Black, 2014).

Outside of the classroom walls, there are many opportunities for students to step into leadership roles within a school community (Edwards, 2018). Students participating in theater or music groups within the school have opportunities to rise to leadership positions that spearhead initiatives and guide students towards success in these activities. Students can join clubs that encourage them to lead fundraising efforts or coordinate events schoolwide. Some students may choose to join athletic teams and earn the title of captain, leading their group through a sports season. Importantly, many experts note that effective leadership requires a great deal of self-reflection (Edwards, 2018). Students must consider their actions, biases, and behaviors after they occur, and plan actionable ways in which to improve. This can be done alone or with a trusted adult, but requires critical thinking skills, as well as maturity and self-actualization (Edwards, 2018). Equity education calls for all students to rise to leadership roles within a school community; within the walls of a classroom is only one way in which to do this (Cruz & Stake, 2012).

Gender, Sexuality, and Student Leadership

Historically, leadership has been defined by predominantly white, privileged men as a masculine endeavor (Haber-Curran & Tillapaugh, 2017). Because accepted views of leadership have been hierarchical and tied to power and privilege for centuries, people from underrepresented groups have historically not connected with, and have even resisted, leadership as a personal endeavor (Komives & Dugan, 2010). Shifts in societal thinking have led to several movements where female leaders have emerged in the past century, and educators and scholars in the field of education are working to advance the dialogue about women and girls in leadership roles (Hill, Miller, Benson, & Handley, 2016). In equity education, more female students, as well as students who identify as a gender outside of the binary norm, must be encouraged and supported in their quest to accept and thrive in leadership roles (Hill et al., 2016). Girls must be encouraged to step into roles and assume leadership titles that, in the past, have been primarily held by boys such as class president and school council (Hill et al., 2016. Individuals who identify outside the gender normative must see leaders that are representative of themselves; this, in turn, will encourage those individuals to pursue opportunities to lead (Jourian & Simmons, 2017).

Students whose sexuality differs from a heterosexual preference must be encouraged to seek out and successfully attain leadership roles (Zane, 2018). The role of equity education is to level the playing field for all students so that successful results, both academic and social-emotional, may be achieved by all. Students of varying sexual preference must be included in this conversation. Students who identify as gay, lesbian, bisexual or any other sexual identity, must be actively and explicitly encouraged to step into leadership roles (Zane, 2018). In an educational setting, students should see trusted educators who are representative of themselves; they must connect to professionals who are communicative and standing up in leadership positions.

In addition to sexuality differences, women and girls have a lower self-efficacy in their ability for leadership; much of the research indicates that women receive messages from a young age that women and men are 'supposed' to lead in different ways (Haber-Curran & Zulpilio, 2017). This is troublesome for many reasons, but primarily because it perpetuates outdated myths and further ostracizes marginalized groups.

Final Thoughts

The field of education as a whole must endure a constant barrage of change and scrutiny on an evolving basis. Public education in this country is charged with the enormous task of providing a fair and equitable education for all students, all while battling difficult realities of biased funding and deteriorating family units, among many other pressing issues. Those at the forefront of educational policy making often appear divided in how to best serve this nation's children. Nonetheless, the concept of equity education has risen to the forefront of best practices, and states and districts around the country are working diligently to ascertain the best ways in which to deliver this equity to all students.

The ways in which the goals of equity education are met vary between states and districts, often with local leadership putting priority or funding on specific initiatives that support students. Specifically, administrators have autonomy to decide upon programs that foster student leadership programs, such as peer mentorship initiatives or service learning projects. Research clearly indicates that schools should be encouraging leadership programs that explicitly teach both hard and soft leadership skills to students, especially to those from marginalized groups. This focus on equity assures that all students, regardless of socioeconomic status, academic ability, sexual orientation, race, or religion have access to leadership-building opportunities. Students of color, students with sexual or gender orientation outside the binary norm, and female students should be actively and explicitly recruited into leadership roles.

It is critically important for students to see themselves represented in the leaders they encounter on an everyday basis. Students should see teachers, administrators, community leaders, and others that look and sound like them, that they can relate to, and that will champion efforts to offer programs that foster their growth and development. The principles of equity education are the underpinning of modern social change and equity education is a critical catalyst for modern leadership development.

Points to Remember

- *Equity education is a relatively new concept in the complex mosaic of education in the United States.*
- *Equity education levels the playing field; students receive what they need to be successful, and not all students receive the same thing.*
- *Leadership is a skill that can be cultivated and improved upon, similar to any other academic or social concept.*

- Equity education calls for all students to have equal access to leadership development activities and programs, regardless of social, academic or economic need.
- The most effective strategies for leadership development are teacher modeling, adult/student relationship-building, mentoring, and service learning. These lead students to develop with an equity framework.

References

The Aspen Institute. (2018). *Pursuing social and emotional development through a racial lens: A call to action.* Retrieved from https://assets.aspeninstitute.org/content/uploads/2018/05/Aspen-Institute_Framing-Doc_Call-to-Action.pdf

Balikci, A. (2018). An examination of educational and familial factors in leadership development. *Universal Journal of Educational Research, 6,* 265–271. Retrieved from https://eric.ed.gov/?id=EJ1170602

Black, R., Walsh, L., Hutchins, L., Berman, N. & Groundwater-Smith, S. (2014). *Student leadership: A review of effective practice.* Retrieved from https://education.nsw.gov.au/student-wellbeing/media/documents/attendance-behaviour-engagement/engagement/StudLead_LitReview_fullrpt.pdf

Blazar, D. & Kraft, M.A. (2017). Teacher and teaching effects on students' attitudes and behaviors. *Educational Evaluation and Policy Analysis. 39*(1), 146-170. DOI: 10.3102/0162373716670260

Bowen, J. (2014). Emotion in the Classroom: An Update. *To Improve the Academy.* 33(2), 96-219. DOI:10.1002/tia2.20012

Carnicelli, S. & Boluk, K. (2017). The promotion of social justice: Service learning for transformative education. *Journal of hospitality, leisure, sport & tourism education, 21*(B), 126-134. DOI: 10.1016/j.jhlste.2017.01.003

Clark, D. (2017). *Developing leadership qualities in the classroom through SEL.* Retrieved from https://www.gettingsmart.com/2017/01/developing-leadership-qualities-through-sel/

Cruz, F., & Stake, R. E. (2012). Teaching about equity, learning about discrimination in a meritocratic society. *Qualitative Research in Education, 1,* 112–134. Retrieved from https://files.eric.ed.gov/fulltext/EJ1114051.pdf

Doyle, A. (2018). *Top 10 leadership skills.* Retrieved from https://www.thebalancecareers.com/top-leadership-skills-2063782

Edwards, B. (2018). *Student leadership is fundamental to positive school climate.* Retrieved from https://www.amle.org/BrowsebyTopic/WhatsNew/WNDet/TabId/270/ArtMID/888/ArticleID/920/Student-Leadership-is-Fundamental-to-Positive-School-Climate.aspx

Elmore, T. (2017). *The fastest trick to develop student leaders.* Retrieved from https://growingleaders.com/blog/fastest-trick-develop-student-leaders/

Gonzales, D., & Weiner, R. (2017, May 31). Our schools have an equity problem. What should we do about it? *Education Week.* Retrieved from https://www.edweek.org/ew/articles/2017/05/31/our-schools-have-an-equity-problem-what.html

Haber-Curran, P., & Tillapaugh, D. (2017). Gender and student leadership: A critical examination. In D. Tillapaugh & P. Haber-Curran (Eds.), *New directions for student leadership: Vol. 154. Critical perspectives on gender and student leadership* (pp. 11–22). San Francisco, CA: Jossey-Bass.

Haber-Curran, P. & Sulpizio, L. (2017). Student leadership development for girls and young women. In D. Tillapaugh & P. Haber-Curran (Eds.), *New directions for student leadership: Critical perspectives on gender and student leadership* (pp. 33-46). San Francisco, CA: Jossey-Bass.

Haber-Curran, P. & Tillapaugh, D. (2017). Gender and student leadership: A critical examination. In D. Tillapaugh & P. Haber-Curran (Eds.), *New directions for student leadership: Critical perspectives on gender and student leadership* (pp. 11-22). San Francisco, CA: Jossey-Bass.

Hill, C., Miller, K., Benson, K., & Handley, G. (2016). Barriers and bias: The status of women in leadership. *American Association of University Women.* Retrieved from https://www.aauw.org/aauw_check/pdf_download/show_pdf.php?file=barriers-and-bias

Jourian, T.J. & Simmons, S.L. (2017). Trans*Leadership. In D. Tillapaugh & P. Haber-Curran (Eds.), *New directions for student leadership: Critical perspectives on gender and student leadership* (pp. 59-70). San Francisco, CA: Jossey-Bass.

Komives, S. R., & Dugan, J. P. (2014). Student leadership development: Theory, research, and practice. In D. V. Day (Ed.), *Oxford library of psychology: The Oxford handbook of leadership and organizations* (pp. 805–831). New York, NY: Oxford University Press.

Lund, D.E. (2018). *The Wiley international handbook of service-learning for social justice.* Hoboken, NJ: John Wiley & Sons.

Masters, G. (2018). What is 'equity' in education? *Teacher Magazine.* Retrieved from https://www.teachermagazine.com.au/columnists/geoff-masters/what-is-equity-in-education

Musu-Gillette, L., de Brey, C., McFarland, J., Hussar, W., Sonnenberg, W., & Wilkinson-Flicker, S. (2017). *Status and trends in the education of racial and ethnic groups 2017* (NCES 2017-051). Washington, DC: U.S. Department of Education, National Center for Education Statistics. Retrieved from https://nces.ed.gov/pubsearch/pubsinfo.asp?pubid=2017051.

National Equity Project. (2017). National Equity Project. Retrieved from http://nationalequityproject.org

Rimmer, J. (n.d.), *Developing principals as equity-centered instructional leaders.* Retrieved from https://capacitybuildingnetwork.org/article9/

Starmans, C., Sheskin, M., & Bloom, P. (2017). Why people prefer unequal societies. *Nature Human Behavior, 1*(4), 82. DOI: 10.1038/s41562-017-0082

Taylor, R., Smiley, L., & Richards, S. (2015). *Exceptional Students*. New York, NY: McGraw Hill.

United Nations Educational, Scientific, and Cultural Organization. (2017). *A guide for ensuring inclusion and equity in education.* Retrieved from http://unesdoc.unesco.org/images/0024/002482/248254e.pdf

Walker, T. (2013). *Is America ready to talk about equity in education?* Retrieved from http://neatoday.org/2013/05/28/is-america-ready-to-talk-about-equity-in-education-2/

Winch, G. (2015). Can leadership be learned or are you born with it? *Psychology Today.* Retrieved from https://www.psychologytoday.com/us/blog/the-squeaky-wheel/201502/can-leadership-be-learned-or-are-you-born-it

Zane, Z. (2018). *New Study: Businesses perform better with LGBTQ individuals in leadership roles.* Retrieved from https://www.out.com/news-opinion/2018/8/14/businesses-perform-better-lgbtq-individuals-leadership-roles

Chapter Nine
Extracurricular Activities: Promoting Equity Outside the Classroom

Micheline S. Malow, *Manhattanville College*

Although children spend a significant amount of time in the classroom setting, between six and eight hours a day, five days a week, school hours do not align with the typical working hours of parents and caregivers (Musu-Gillette, de Brey, McFarland, Hussar, Sonnenberg, & Wilkinson-Flicker, 2017). Furthermore, the complexities of modern life necessitate that the majority of adults who care for children in a household setting (loosely conceived of as a family) are gainfully employed to support the family unit. This schedule discrepancy leaves families with the need to manage the several hours after school that children have without prescribed responsibilities and fill them in ways that are both meaningful and supportive (Marcoux, 2018).

Feeling required to manage children's out of school hours has soared in response to the rise in two-parent and single-parent working families over the last five decades in the United States (Pew Research Center, 2015). As this phenomenon developed into the norm, the term 'latchkey' children was coined to describe the experience of children returning home before their parents returned from work; however, the negative connotations associated with latchkey children propelled families to push for community responses to safely and productively manage children's out of school time (Blakemore, 2015).

Children and Free Time

To address questions of children's out of school time, Larson and Verma (1999) examined the ways in which children around the world spent their time. Results from this investigation found that children in post-industrialized societies managed free time in ways that varied but corresponded to parents' values and socioeconomic status (SES) (Larson & Verma, 1999). Children throughout Asia frequently spent their free hours in more schoolwork, while children in North America spent their time on leisure activities (Larson & Verma, 1999). The researchers noted that there were specific variables, such as gender, age and SES that impacted how children spent their time, and the engagement in specific activities reinforced the family's developmental goals for the children (Larson & Verma, 1999). Those families, for example, concerned about their children's future employment had children engage in academic activity; after school hours engaged in academic pursuits led to high achievement and long-term economic productivity, although in the short-term children experienced lower intrinsic motivation (Larson & Verma, 1999). Conversely, engagement in leisure activity during free-time increased student self-direction, yet it did not necessarily enhance long-term economic prospects. The difference in activity choice reflects the familial values imbued in free-time activities.

Currently, most parents have options of how to manage children's free time, although the number of choices depends on where the family resides due to different educational mandates and whether the family is in a rural, suburban, or urban area (Pew Research Center, 2015). Although these options exist in response to demonstrated need, it does not mean that all families want or have access to the available options in their community. Specifically, Larson and Verma (1999) indicated that "material conditions, normative patterns, and cultural values" (p. 728) are considerations that families deliberate when making decisions about children's free time. Huebner and Mancini (2003) stated that "In many respects family values, interests, and capacities control the access that youth have to activity participation, especially when they are younger" (p. 460). These researchers recognized that there remain many discrepancies in regard to how children's free time is managed; for example, all societies display hierarchical systems that expose difficulties experienced by non-dominant groups. Dominant groups within societies often have access to rights, social capital, and material resources that non-dominant groups may not be able to access (Corning, 2011). This means that by the luck of the birth lottery, members of a particular society's dominant group have opportunities for success that outnumber those of the non-dominant group.

Legitimation of Social Inequality

Costa-Lopes, Dovido, Pereira, and Jost (2013) contend that "the stability of inequality is remarkable" (p. 229) given that justice, cooperation, and reciprocity are necessary components of successful societies. These researchers noted that disparities in capitalistic societies are increasing.

This view substantiates the adage that the rich get richer while the poor get poorer. Reasons for the continuity of inequality has been considered by social scientists for decades, with principles of 'legitimation' factoring prominently in understanding inequality. Legitimation is the "social and psychological processes by which attitudes, behaviors, and social arrangements are justified as conforming to normative standards – including, but not limited to – standards of justice" (Costa-Lopes et al., 2013, p.230).

Social scientists believe that individuals, groups, and societies all engage in the process of legitimation; shaping the beliefs of those who benefit most from upholding the social system and substantiating the 'status quo' (Costa-Lopes et al., 2013). These same processes shape the beliefs of non-dominant groups allowing for the maintenance of social systems and policies; thus, legitimation perpetuates social disparities by defending the system's merits and modulating the system's flaws. Although processes of legitimation maintain inequality, those same processes are thought to also propel societal change; making legitimation a double-edged sword (Costa-Lopes et al., 2013). Legitimization and delegitimization can preserve oppressive systems of social stratification [yet it can also] serve the causes of justice, progress, and social change" (Jost & Major, 2001, p. 12). When examining children's spontaneous activities, spending time with family, friends, or alone, there is little difference between advantaged and disadvantaged families (Muschamp, Bullock, Ridge, & Wikeley, 2009). Everyday activities like shopping, spending time caring for others, watching television or playing on a computer, reading, or just hanging out predominate amongst both groups; however, in an organized societal system, such as the education system, disparities emerge in regard to free time activities (Muschamp et al., 2009).

In the United States (U.S.), federal legislation guarantees each child a free and appropriate public education (FAPE) (U.S. Department of Education, 2010). The 1954 Supreme Court ruling in *Brown vs. the Board of Education*, deemed state-sponsored segregation in public education unconstitutional (Administrative Office of the U.S. Courts, n.d.). This decision determined that the segregation of public schools violated the Equal Protection Clause of the Fourteenth Amendment (Administrative Office of the U.S. Courts, n.d.). Despite this, educational systems continue to be a place where the legitimation of inequality is evident; one needs to look no further than the disparity of school systems in communities that are characterized by high SES and those in communities characterized by families with lower SES.

The difference between the tangibles in SES disparate schools, including the physical plant, the academic resources, and the school-sponsored activities, are just a few of the inequalities experienced by children and families in the different communities (Marshall, 2015). This is even more apparent in a fiscally conservative environment where school 'specials' such as music, art, drama, and sports are taken out of the curriculum offerings due to the expense of running those programs (BBC News, 2015). In place of these enriching activities, children are provided more of what they already spend their school day engaged in – English language arts, math, social studies, and science.

Organizing Children's Activities

Parents in the U.S. and other countries have embraced education as the great equalizer as well as the accepted path to improve future SES potential for their children, and future generations, making academic success a 'high stakes' game. Other post-industrial nations such as England, Taiwan, and Korea, hold similar views demonstrating the powerfully pervasive belief held by nations around the world (Muschamp et al., 2009; Shih & Yi, 2014; Bae, Kim, Lee, Kim, 2009). Coming from this perspective, it is understandable that parents everywhere are searching for ways to give their children a viable advantage. One way to give children a competitive advantage is to utilize the available time, the time not spent in school, to enroll children in activities that are valued by the parents and society (Shih & Yi, 2014). In this regard, activities such as sports, the arts, academic enrichment and other activities are seen as a means for parents to enhance children's social, cognitive, and other capacities (Mahoney, Harris, & Eccles, 2006; Muschamp, et.al., 2009; Shih & Yi, 2014; Bae, et al., 2009).

Organized activities have always been a part of children's lives; however, in the post latchkey children era, the parental programming of children's activities has taken on new importance (Blakemore, 2015). With the growth of children's participation in organized activities, research has studied and demonstrated that, in general, participation in organized activities is associated with positive outcomes for the children (Crosnoe, Smith, Leventhal, 2015; Simpkins, Ripke, Huston, & Eccles, 2005). With the value that parents' have imparted onto scheduling their children's time, big business has followed with a proliferation of educational institutes and 'schools' providing instruction on various leisure activities (Shih & Yi, 2014).

Private companies have grown to fill the void and to serve the various needs of families (Grossman, Lind, Hayes, McMaken, & Gersick, 2009). In this way, working parents of young children enter into this social system by paying others to arrange for the supervision and enrichment of their children through childcare. As children grow, enrichment classes can be booked to enhance or to replace curriculum that may not be provided or is lost in school due to other priorities (Grossman et al., 2009). As children gain knowledge and expertise in selected areas, private lessons and tutors can provide the learning opportunities to further advantage the children. In this way, parenting practices can be seen as a factor in social reproduction, the linkage of parental values, social class, and children's activity participation (Shih & Yi, 2014).

One problem with relying on private companies to enrich children's lives is that it fosters further disparity among the economically advantaged and disadvantaged groups of a society (Grossman et al., 2009; Wong, 2015). Children of economically advantaged families are able to benefit from the proliferation of private companies providing academic enrichment, sports, the arts, or other desired activities because they are willing and able to pay for the services being provided; however, those families from lower SES backgrounds may not be able to afford to pay for the advantage of the out-of-school enriching activities, thereby widening family-related social and economic disparities (Grossman et al., 2009; Marshall, 2015; Wong, 2015).

In order to address this concern and fill the need the private companies serve, public schools and community/religious based programs have developed programs that incorporate structured activities that are no cost or low-cost to the students enrolled (Wong, 2015). In this way, parents' options have expanded, allowing families to choose from a bevy of affordable out-of-school and after-school activities. Despite this move to provide organized, structured activities for children from low SES backgrounds, inequality persists. Examination of enrollment data show that children from low SES families are more likely to attend school-based after-school or community/religious based programs, while children from economically advantaged households continue to be enrolled in private programs (Bae et al., 2009; Simpkins et al., 2005).

Participation in organized activities, both out-of-school and after-school, has been examined to evaluate the benefit provided to the children engaged in the various types of activities (Marshall, 2015). Structured activities are usually supervised by an adult and include, but are not limited to, volunteer work, clubs, religious organization activities, academic enrichment, and arts-based activities (e.g., art, drama, music lessons, etc.) (Crosnoe et al., 2015). One study sought to capture activity participation histories of children and explore how those histories impacted academic achievement at the start of high school (Crosnoe et al., 2015). The researchers posited that there were important transition times in a child's life that activity participation would advantage such as elementary school to middle school and middle school to high school (Crosnoe et al., 2015). For this investigation, the researchers gathered information about structured activity participation from mothers during first through fifth grade, then the children reported on their own structured activity participation in ninth grade (Crosnoe et al., 2015). Gender, SES, GPA, and other social variables, in addition to the grade level associated with the critical transition times, were gathered as well.

Surprisingly, by ninth grade more than nine out of ten students reported involvement in at least one kind of structured activity (Crosnoe et al., 2015). Moreover, consistent activity participation throughout the years of schooling was associated with higher academic achievement at the start of high school (Crosnoe et al., 2015). Results from this investigation found that children who had either consistent participation, whether they started the activity early in elementary school and continued with it, or began the activity later in elementary school but persisted, had a greater grade point average (GPA) by 97% of a standard deviation over non-participators in ninth grade; thus, both the duration and timing of engagement in activities was found to be important to GPA (Crosnoe et al., 2015).

Results suggested that the consistent participators and latecomers tended to be girls and to come from socially advantaged neighborhoods; however, children from disadvantaged families that were classified as latecomers to an activity, meaning they started participating in the activity late in elementary school, also benefited academically from engagement in an organized, structured activity (Crosnoe et al., 2015). Although any kind of participation was found to be positively associated with increased GPA in this investigation, those children who had participated in the organized activity since elementary school evidenced the most positive outcomes (Crosnoe et al., 2015).

In an effort to understand what predicts an adolescent's use of free time, Huebner and Mancini (2003) explored the correlates of structured activities for both out-of-school and after-school programs. To determine the factors involved with the utilization of free time, the researchers utilized multiple variables associated with the self (e.g. gender, ethnicity, grade, and academic achievement), with family factors (e.g. SES, family structure, and family processes such as endorsement of an activity), as well as factors associated with friends (e.g. peer pressure, peer activity engagement, etc.) as predictors of participation in structured activities (Huebner & Mancini, 2003). Several findings emerged; specifically, for after-school activities variables of parental endorsement, ethnicity, and friend endorsement were significant (Huebner & Mancini, 2003). For out-of-school activities variables of peer pressure, parent endorsement, and high academic achievement were significant as was parental endorsement, or support, for the activity in which the children were enrolled (Huebner & Mancini, 2003). Gender was found to be an important factor for greater participation in religious activities, with girls participating more than boys (Huebner & Mancini, 2003). Ethnicity, children identifying as African American, was seen to be important for participation in after-school activities as well as in religious activities (Huebner & Mancini, 2003). There was a positive relationship between grade level and volunteer activities, with a significant association with SES (Huebner & Mancini, 2003). When children from economically advantaged families reached the upper grades in high school, they engaged in significantly more volunteer activities, often seen as a way to try out careers or as a boost for college applications.

After-School and Out-of-School Activities

Organized, out-of-school activities can provide children with enriching social, cognitive and personal opportunities. A growing body of research finds that children's participation in structured activities after the school day has ended is associated with both academic achievement and well-being (Simpkins et al., 2005; Muschamp et al., 2009). One study examined whether structured activities in a community setting could compensate for imbalances in the school curriculum (Muschamp et al., 2009). In this investigation, early adolescent children's dispositions were qualitatively analyzed to examine vulnerabilities, identities, experiences, understanding, and involvement in the structured activity (Muschamp et al., 2009). The provision of free school meals served as a proxy variable for SES and the researchers found that although both economically advantaged and low SES children participated in structured activities, the variety and the number of structured activities differed (Muschamp et al., 2009). In sixth grade, advantaged children participated in art, music, drama, and sports; however, while low SES children also participated in structured activities, they mainly participated in activities provided through the school (Muschamp et al., 2009). In this study, the difference found in the participation gap increased by ninth grade as low SES children reduced participation in structured activities and engaged in a narrower range of activities (Muschamp et al., 2009). Researchers found that children from low SES families demonstrated a lack of knowledge of what was possible for them in regard to access and cost of structured activities in the community.

Key factors identified as barriers to participation for children from low SES families in this investigation included the cost of attending the organized activities, transportation, availability of facilities, and responsibilities in the home (Muschamp et al., 2009). Further complicating the dispositions of the children was the identity development that economically disadvantaged children missed out on. Membership in an activity and the community of practice that surrounds the organized activity was found to provide a positive learning identity for those children able to engage in the organized activities. For economically disadvantaged children, a negative learning identity emerged as a result of non-participation; the vulnerability experienced by the children surfaced as a strategy of self-exclusion; thus, the physical barriers to out-of-school activities experienced by economically disadvantaged children turned into psychological barriers, limiting the potential for future engagement (Muschamp et al., 2009).

Final Thoughts

Parents and caregivers want the economic opportunities that the world has to offer to be available to their children. Education has been put forth as the great equalizer, enabling movement between social classes. However, the typical educational programming is no longer thought to be sufficient; if a little education is good, then more must be better! This thinking, coinciding with the increase of two-parent and single-parent working households, has propelled parents to take up the task of managing their children's free time.

Children's free time, after-school hours, and weekends are now more organized and scheduled to provide maximum social, cognitive, and skill development. Educational companies and learning professionals have saturated communities in an effort to provide opportunities for academic enhancement, language development, sports training, and engagement with the arts (e.g., music, drama, visual art). Education as big business is available to all children, as long as their family has the ability to pay for the services.

Inequality in after-school educational practices has now become common; economically advantaged families are able to provide high quality valued knowledge and skills that give advantage to children as they move toward adulthood. However, low SES families are not able to advantage children in this way, increasing the inequity. As a means to address the imbalance, school-, community-, and religious-based programs have proliferated. Low SES families now have more educational enrichment opportunities available for their children, although as governmental funding for these programs waxes and wanes, the opportunities and quality of the programs may suffer.

Researchers have investigated the impact of organized, structured activities on children's development and have concluded that, in general, participation in after-school and out-of-school activities bestows positive benefits. Economic realities of modern living ensure that work-life balance complications for parents will continue; therefore, school – activity scheduling for children is also sure to continue. Providing organized, structured, high-quality activity opportunities to all children is a needed focus for educational systems.

Points to Remember

- *Structured activities, both in and out of school, are important for social integration, as well as for children's cognitive and skill development; however, engagement in structured activities related to religious affiliation may not be a discretionnary activity for some children, although participation in the activity may still provide social and cognitive benefit.*
- *Family SES is a barrier to free time activities for children from low SES families. Family finances determine whether there is money to participate in structured activities, whether there is transportation available to get the children to the activity, whether other family responsibilities interfere with participation in out-of-school activities, and whether the family values the potential advantages that the activity offers.*
- *Activities are not mere distractions to student achievement. To the contrary, enriching activities actually serve as academic support, keeping children engaged in the school setting. The challenge is to provide quality after-school experiences that provide both physical access to a variety of structured activities, but also provide psychological access for identity development.*
- *Waning public investment in school-based extracurricular activities is counterproductive. Schools are best able to provide consistent participation for children from disadvantaged families due to the barrier of high cost of participation outside of the school setting.*
- *Activity participation tailored to engage specific groups of students, such as those from economically disadvantaged homes, are in the best position to promote sustained and consistent activity participation. Consistent activity partici-*

pation promotes the level of skill development and automaticity that is necessary in order for positive, generalized benefits to emerge.

References

Administrative Office of the U.S. Courts. (n.d.). History-Brown v. Board of Education re-enactment. Retrieved from http://www.uscourts.gov/educational-resources/educational-activities/history-brown-v-board-education-re-enactment

BBC News. (2015). Arts and creativity 'squeezed out of schools.' Retrieved from https://www.bbc.com/news/education-31518717

Bae, S.H., Kim, H., Lee, C.W., & Kim, H.W. (2009). The relationship between after-school program participation and student's demographic background. *KEDI Journal of Educational Policy, 6* (2), 69-96. Retrieved from https://www.researchgate.net/publication/287731946_The_relationship_between_after-school_program_participation_and_student's_demographic_background

Blakemore, E. (2015). *The latchkey generation: How bad was it?* Retrieved from https://daily.jstor.org/latchkey-generation-bad/

Corning, P. (2011). *The fair society: The science of human nature and the pursuit of social justice.* Chicago, IL: University of Chicago Press.

Costa-Lopes, R., Dovido, J.F., Pereira, C.R., & Jost, J.T. (2013). Social psychological perspectives on the legitimation of social inequality: Past, present and future. *European Journal of Social Psychology, 43*(4), 229-237. DOI: 10.1002/ejsp.1966

Crosnoe, R., Smith, C., & Leventhal, T. (2015). Family background, school-age trajectories of activity participation, and academic achievement at the start of high school. *Applied Developmental Science, 19*(3), 1-14. DOI: 10.1080/10888691.2014.983031

Grossman, J.B., Lind, C., Hayes, C., McMaken, J., & Gersick A. (2009). *The cost of quality out-of-school-time programs.* Retrieved from https://www.wallacefoundation.org/knowledge-center/Documents/The-Cost-of-Quality-of-Out-of-School-Time-Programs.pdf

Huebner, A.J., & Mancini, J.A. (2003). Shaping structured out-of-school time use among youth: The effects of self, family, and friend systems. *Journal of Youth and Adolescence, 32*(6), 453-463. DOI: 10.1023/A:1025990419215

Jost, J.T., & Major, B. (2001). Emerging perspectives on the psychology of legitimacy. In J.T. Jost, & B. Major (Eds.). *The psychology of legitimacy: Emerging perspectives on ideology, justice, and intergroup relations* (pp. 3-30). New York, NY: Cambridge University Press.

Larson, R.W., & Verma, S. (1999). How children and adolescents spend time across the world: Work, play, and developmental opportunities.

Psychological Bulletin, 125(6), 701-736. DOI: 10.1037/0033-2909.125.6.701

Mahoney, J.L., Harris, A.L., & Eccles, J.S. (2006). Organized activity participation, positive youth development, and the over-scheduling hypothesis. *SRCD Social Policy Reports, 20*(4), 3-15. Retrieved from https://eric.ed.gov/?id=ED521752

Marcoux, H. (2018). *There's a childcare gap after school-and it's hurting families.* Retrieved from https://www.mother.ly/news/after-school-care-gap-working-parents

Marshall, J.D. (2015). *Is there an academic benefit to participating in extracurricular activities: A systemic review and meta-analysis.* Retrieved from http://wp.cune.org/jillmarshall/files/2015/02/Is-there-an-Academic-Benefit-to-Participating-in-Extracurricular-Activities-A-Systemic-Review-and-Meta-analysis.pdf

Muschamp, Y., Bullock, K., Ridge, T., Wikeley, F. (2009). 'Nothing to do': The impact of poverty on pupils' learning identities within out-of-school activities. *British Educational Research Journal, 35* (2), 305-321. DOI: 10:1080/01411920802044362

Musu-Gillette, L., de Brey, C., McFarland, J., Hussar, W., Sonnenberg, W., & Wilkinson-Flicker, S. (2017). *Status and trends in the education of racial and ethnic groups 2017* (NCES 2017-051). Washington, DC: U.S. Department of Education, National Center for Education Statistics. Retrieved from https://nces.ed.gov/pubs2017/2017051.pdf

Pew Research Center. (2015). *Parenting in America.* Retrieved from http://www.pewsocialtrends.org/2015/12/17/parenting-in-america/

Shih, Y.P., & Yi, C.C. (2014). Cultivating the difference: Social class, parental values, cultural capital and children's after-school activities in Taiwan. *Journal of Comparative Family Studies, 45*(1), 55-75. Retrieved from https://www.ios.sinica.edu.tw/ios/people/personal/chinyi/CultivatingTheDifferenceInTaiwan.pdf

Simpkins, S.D., Ripke, M., Huston, A.C., & Eccles, J. (2005). Predicting participation and outcomes in out-of-school activities: Similarities and differences across social ecologies. *New Directions for Youth Development, 105,* 51-69. DOI: 10.1002/yd.107

U.S. Department of Education. (2010). *Free Appropriate Public Education.* Retrieved from https://www2.ed.gov/about/offices/list/ocr/docs/edlite-FAPE504.html

Wong, A. (2015). *The activity gap.* Retrieved from https://www.theatlantic.com/education/archive/2015/01/the-activity-gap/384961/

Chapter Ten

Collaboration and Self-Development: Professional Learning to Reduce Bias

Nicholas D. Young, *American International College*

Elizabeth Jean, *Endicott College*

There are approximately 3.8 million public school teachers in the United States and, of these, 80 percent are white, 16 percent are black or Hispanic, and the last five percent are Asian or of mixed race (Walker, 2018). On average, today's educator is a white, middle class, forty-something woman with approximately 14 years of experience and a master's degree (Walker, 2018; Early Childhood Education Degrees, 2018).

America's public schools are home to over 48,633,000 students; just over half of these students are white, while 19,000,000 are black or Hispanic (Statista, 2018). Race, however, is just one defining factor for these students. Black and Hispanic students who attended schools in high poverty areas were greater in number than the national average, while students who were defined as white, Asian, or American/Native were more likely to attend schools in low poverty schools and were fewer in number than the national average (National Center for Education Statistics, 2018). In the 2015-2016 school year, some 40 percent of students resided in cities where there were high-poverty schools; thus, they were considered students who lived in poverty (National Center for Education Statistics, 2018).

These are important statistics when attempting to define where personal bias might exist and how such an educator might mitigate the effects of such powerful negative thinking. If most teachers are white, middle-class females and they teach in high poverty schools where the majority of students are of color, it behooves them to take a critical eye inward to examine biases they might not even be aware of. Personal development, therefore, is necessary for all educators as they implement a social justice framework in their classroom.

Understanding White Privilege

In a ground-breaking article, McIntosh (1988) offered a personal reflection of white privilege. Its effects were immediate and far-reaching, and to this day, it is used as a measure of consideration in professional/personal development and diversity classes. McIntosh (1988) saw that many whites, herself included, operated from a "base of unacknowledged privilege" (n.p.) and that as a white woman, she too enjoyed "unearned skin privilege" (n.p.). McIntosh (1988) listed 46 things that set her apart from those with different skin tone and SES; these daily experiences were taken for granted and were part of an "invisible package of unearned assets" (McIntosh, 1988, n.p.).

To understand that this was a much more prevalent bias was eye-opening to McIntosh (1988) who described the realization:

> *In my place and class, I did not see myself as a racist because I was taught to recognize racism as only individual acts of meanness by members of my group, never in invisible systems conferring unsought racial dominance on my group from birth* (McIntosh, 1989, n.p.).

That paper was the beginning of a life-long courtship with social activism that led to the founding of The National SEED Project (2018), whose mission it is to seek "educational equity and diversity [through] peer-led professional development" (n.p.). Using a 'train the trainer' model, individuals are taught to facilitate seminars in which personal testimony and reflection, in combination with experiential learning, offers a bridge to "acknowledge systems of oppression, power, and privilege" (The National SEED Project, 2018, n.p.).

Defining Bias and Prejudice

Bias is a "function of the human condition" (Jana, as cited in Kruse, 2017, n.p.). Everyone uses bias as a means to decision-making; for example, preferring clothes that are colorful as opposed to monotone. The problem with bias occurs when it is focused on federally recognized protected classes to include age, disability, gender, national origin, pregnancy/sex, race/color, religion, and veteran status (A&E Television Networks: History, 2018).

Bias is defined as "an inclination of temperament or outlook, *especially:* a personal and sometimes unreasoned judgement" (Merriam-Webster, 2018a). Interestingly, the same source offers this definition "a tendency to believe that some people, ideas, etc., are better than others that usually results in treating some people unfairly" (Merriam-Webster, 2018a).

Prejudice is defined as "an irrational attitude of hostility directed against an individual, a group, a race, or their supposed characteristics" (Merriam-Webster, 2018b). It is the exclusion of a person or groups of persons based on false beliefs. With these definitions in mind, personal bias is unique to each individual. It is a preconception or a prejudice that is founded on a lack of understanding and it is within the individual's wheelhouse to change. When the individual is part of a majority group, the "accumulated unconscious bias" (Suttie, 2016, n.p.) can be even more destructive.

Using these definitions in combination with the idea that bias is often unrecognized and/or not acknowledged, and the statistics mentioned previously, it stands to reason that there might be some natural, unconscious bias when the majority of the teaching force are white, middle-class women who primarily teach students of color and low SES. For this reason, through self-development, recognizing and acknowledging privilege and bias, and coming to terms with it, is the first step in allowing social justice to exist in the classroom and school in a way that truly honors all students.

Implicit Bias

Implicit bias is more difficult to see as it "is subtle, unconscious, or hard to pin down" (Miller, 2016, n.p.). Implicit bias has been likened to a habit; once an individual is aware of it, s/he is able to change it. A recent study determined that unconscious bias exists in most people, and teachers were no exception (Suttie, 2016). In one experiment, teachers were asked to watch a video in which black and white students played together with the task of looking for behavioral issues (there were none); however, the adults spent less time staring at the white children - as if their preconceived notion was that the black children were more likely to misbehave (Suttie, 2016).

In another experiment within the same study, teachers were tasked with reading passages about children who were experiencing a behavioral challenge (Suttie, 2016). They were identified only as a white girl, black girl, white boy, or black boy and in some cases, the teacher was given background information. The experiment found that when the student was of a different race than the teacher, the discipline was more severe, leading to the conclusion that individuals are "more inclined to punish those who look different from us" (Suttie, 2016, n.p.). Even more startling, black boys are statistically more likely to be reprimanded than any other group (Balingit, 2018).

Yet another study looked to reduce implicit race bias through intervention. This twelve- week study offered an intervention that was based on a triad approach of awareness, concern, and the application of reduction strategies (Devine, Forscher, Austin, & Cox, 2012). The results indicated that those "who received the intervention showed dramatic reductions in implicit race bias" (Devine et al., 2012, 1267). This proves that educators have the ability to recognize bias in themselves and others and use a proactive approach of concern and positive practices to eliminate the negative effects of bias in the classroom.

Combating Prejudice and Bias in Self

There are many ways to combat negativity and improve personal understanding of protected classes in individuals. As educators, professional development is a normal part of the work that occurs several times a year. Often, administration dictates the necessary learning that will take place based on data collected throughout the prior school year, or during the current school year. They may bring in an expert on prejudice or bias and have educators go through a sensitivity training (Rinderle, 2018). The expectation is that this will be brought back to the class and implemented into daily practice. While this is one way to focus on decreasing unwanted behaviors and habits, there are many others that may prove to be more fruitful and personally impactful.

Mentoring and Coaching

At the institutional or administrative level, providing coaches, mentors, and/or supervision often leads to educator growth. Here, the emphasis is on catching the bias or prejudice as it occurs, then talking about it and finding ways to eliminate the bias and replace it with equity and inclusion. There are four ingredients to a well-developed model to include motivation, ability, awareness, and opportunity (Tennyson, n.d.a). Mentors/coaches should ask open-ended questions such as "When you say X, do you mean…" or "It sounds like…" or "I get the impression that…" (Tennyson, n.d.b). Using active listening skills will ensure that the conversation stays positive and provides a basis for learning. As Tennyson (n.d.b) states, "mentoring is a reciprocal relationship, and it can be very valuable to both you and your mentee if you approach your sessions with an equal dose of empathy and self-awareness" (n.p.).

Bibliotherapy

Bibliotherapy dates back to 1916 and is defined as the use of books to help people recover from issues they experience (American Library Association, 2018, n.p.). While an individual can easily go to the bookstore or library and choose a book on a related topic, in its purest form, a trained bibliotherapist would first meet with a client to ascertain the issues at hand and then prescribe a list of books that met with the appropriate criteria. To focus on prejudice and bias, an individual or therapist might choose books by Nelson Mandela. The books are meant to inspire the reader, resulting in a catharsis, and solution (Ogden, 2016; American Library Association, 2018). According to Ogden (2016), books provide high levels of engagement and

> *enhances our ability to empathize with others, to put ourselves into another's shoes; to become more intuitive about other people's feelings (as well as our own), and to self-reflect on our problems as we read about and empathize with a fictional character who is facing similar problems* (n.p.).

Online Courses

Educators can access online webinars and Massive Online Open Courses (MOOCs) that are specifically related to an area of interest or need. School administration may ask educators to take a survey and, based on the results, choose from a predetermined list of offerings. Alternately, a teacher may decide to become more culturally or personally sensitive to the students in her classroom and independently look for an online course.

Online Webinars. Teaching Tolerance, a project of the Southern Poverty Law Center (2018) offers webinars on a variety of topics to include bullying and bias, class, gender and sexual identity, immigration, race and ethnicity, religion, rights and activism, and slavery. Webinars are generally an hour long and certificates are given at the time of completion.

MOOCs. Massive Open Online Courses allow learners to access college course content at any given time, without cost. One of the largest supplies of MOOCs, edX.org (2018), offers courses such as unconscious bias from over 130 global partners including several well-known post-secondary institutions, while MOOC List (2017) provides a comprehensive listing of courses from a variety of institutions such as ethics in education, diversity and inclusion, as well as gender and sexuality. With both sites, students can earn a certificate at the time of completion and some courses give the option to become a trainer.

Travel

Mark Twain (as cited in Dolan, 2013) once wrote that "travel is fatal to prejudice, bigotry, and narrow-mindedness" (n.p.). It appears that a series of five new studies proves that travel and interactions with others unknown, does indeed eliminate prejudice and "broaden the mind" (Dolan, 2013, n.p.). The studies confirmed that it is the number of diverse experiences, not the depth or length of them, that allow individuals to generalize the trust of others thereby diminishing bias and prejudice (Dolan, 2013).

In order for educators to engage in travel, they must carve out time during the summer months or vacations, choose unusual destinations, and seek out activities and places that provide a culturally immersive experience (Wolz, 2017). Speaking with native-speakers and learning about the culture first-hand provide a balanced experience that leads to better understanding and acceptance (Wolz, 2017).

Home Visits

Home visits provide a platform to learn about a family without judgment. Spending even a brief period of time with others encourages open communication. When the focus is based on understanding others, rather than academics, families often feel more comfortable (Parent Home Visit Project, 2016). During some home visits, the family will offer the visitor a meal; this is a chance to learn another culture, understand family dynamics, and become an advocate for both student and family. The importance of sharing a meal is undeniable, as it builds relationships that transfer into the classroom (Delistraty, 2014). Communication is key and home visits provide the way.

Combating Prejudice and Bias in the Classroom

Teachers have the ability and responsibility to diminish or vanquish unconscious personal biases and create an atmosphere that is welcoming and accepting of all individuals. Before educators can work with students and families in an equitable fashion, engage in conversations about bias and diversity, and speak openly about acceptance, they need to participate in a daily practice that includes a critical look at "personal cultural biases and assumptions… [and work towards] developing an awareness of personal cultural filters" (Anti-Defamation League, 2012, p. 1). This personal practice dovetails with a classroom practice and produces a space in which prejudice and bias are not acceptable.

In addition to educator self-exploration, the Anti-Defamation League (2012) and Suttie (2016) suggest that every daily practice should include the following classroom practices:

- Comprehensive integration of perspectives and information that are culturally diverse and occur all year long. Provide materials that are inclusive and "do not reinforce existing societal stereotypes" (American Defamation League, 2012, p. 3).
- Understanding and ensuring that maturation of acceptance takes time and begins with group norms, mutual respect and honest conversations.
- Providing an environment that is accepting of mistakes and allows those with unconscious biases the space to recognize and change their assumptions. Modeling "non-defensive responses" (American Defamation League, 2012, p. 2) is vital to the process.
- Intervening when acts of bias occur and educating the individuals to understand the implications. Classrooms must be safe havens where students have the tools to succeed.
- Educators routinely discuss current news articles that show bias or anti-bias with students. Students should see teachers as life-long learners.
- The classroom is a microcosm of the world; therefore, it is important that students have a chance to problem solve and resolve conflicts peacefully, as well as work with "diverse teams and think critically about information" (American Defamation League, 2012, p. 3).
- Share life experiences in which bias has been evident. Educators should use carefully chosen literature to build empathy for others and ensure that the classroom is "a place where students' experiences are not marginalized, trivialized or invalidated" (American Defamation League, 2012, p. 3).
- The home-school connection is a vital part of the anti-bias/prejudice process. Involving families ensures that everyone is committed to the learning process.

- Teachers can encourage students to take a mindful moment during the school day. In a recent study, educators who practice mindfulness, or non-judgmental awareness, were shown to have reduced their own unconscious bias (Suttie, 2016).

Final Thoughts

With almost four million public school teachers in the United States, most of whom are white and middle class, and a student body that is more diverse than ever before, it behooves educators to consider their personal bias and prejudices as well as those of their students. Taking into consideration white privilege, prejudice, and implicit bias, educators are tasked with taking a critical look at what they believe, and how they need to change in order to eliminate negative thoughts and actions in themselves and their classrooms.

Educators have several tools available to them that encourage self-reflection and produce positive changes to include formal professional development, mentoring, bibliotherapy, online courses, travel, and home visits. In each case, the emphasis is on looking inward and removing personal bias and prejudice as it is encountered, replacing it with more positive and open thought processes and responses.

In the classroom, it is up to the educator to eliminate implicit bias and prejudice. This can be accomplished through the self-exploration noted above as well as through a daily practice that includes integration of culturally diverse perspectives and operating within a classroom that is accepting of others, just to name a few. An open and positive home-school connection is a vital step as well. With all these strategies available to educators, there is hope that prejudice and bias can be eradicated and replaced with a peaceful classroom culture that is tolerant of all beliefs and people, regardless of differences.

Points to Remember

- *There is an imbalance between the average teacher and the average student. This requires adults to have a greater understanding of the students before them and how best to teach.*
- *White privilege, or unearned skin privilege, occurs when one individual does not recognize the invisible systems in place.*

- *Acknowledgement of oppression, privilege, and power lead the way to educational diversity and equity.*
- *Bias is a habit that can be changed through recognition and replacement. A mentor or coach can help an educator notice when it occurs and offer suggestions to change the behavior.*
- *Options for educators to remediate personal bias and prejudice include mentoring, online classes, travel, home visits, and bibliotherapy.*
- *In the classroom, educators may consider teaching students how to resolve issues and problem solve peacefully, offering an accepting environment, and sharing life experiences as ways to combat bias and prejudice with students.*
- *Encouraging mindful moments has been proven to reduce unconscious bias in educators and students; thus, improving the classroom culture.*

References

A&E Television Networks: History. (2018). *The Civil Rights Act of 1964.* Retrieved from https://www.history.com/topics/black-history/civil-rights-act

American Library Association. (2018). *Bibliotherapy.* Retrieved from http://www.ala.org/tools/atoz/bibliotherapy

Anti-Defamation League. (2012). *Creating an anti-bias learning environment.* Retrieved from https://www.adl.org/media/2182/download

Balingit, M. (2018). *Racial disparities in school discipline are growing, federal data show.* Retrieved from https://www.washingtonpost.com/local/education/racial-disparities-in-school-discipline-are-growing-federal-data-shows/2018/04/24/67b5d2b8-47e4-11e8-827e-190efaf1f1ee_story.html?utm_term=.707d552959b9

Delistraty, C.C. (2014). *The importance of eating together.* Retrieved from https://www.theatlantic.com/health/archive/2014/07/the-importance-of-eating-together/374256/

Devine, P.G., Forscher, P.S., Austin, A.J., & Cox, W.T.L. (2012). Long-term reduction in implicit race bias: A prejudice habit-breaking intervention. *Journal of Experimental Social Psychology, 48*(6), 1267-1278. DOI: 10.1016/j.jesp.2012.06.003.

Dolan, E.W. (2013). *New study confirms Mark Twain's saying: Travel is fatal to prejudice.* Retrieved from https://www.psypost.org/2013/12/new-study-confirms-mark-twains-saying-travel-is-fatal-to-prejudice-21662

Early Childhood Education Degrees. (2018). *America's typical teacher.* Retrieved from https://www.early-childhood-education-degrees.com/americas-typical-teacher/

EdX. (2018). *Unconscious bias: From awareness to action.* Retrieved from https://www.edx.org/course/unconscious-bias-awareness-action-catalystx-ub1x

Kruse, K. (2017). Can we challenge and overcome our biases? *Forbes.* Retrieved from https://www.forbes.com/sites/kevinkruse/2017/07/17/can-we-challenge-and-overcome-our-biases/#5828ef83310e

McIntosh, P. (1988). *White privilege and male privilege: A personal account of coming to see correspondences through work in women's studies.* Retrieved from https://nationalseedproject.org/white-privilege-and-male-privilege

McIntosh, P. (1989). *White privilege: Unpacking the invisible knapsack.* Retrieved from https://nationalseedproject.org/white-privilege-unpacking-the-invisible-knapsack

Merriam-Webster. (2018a). *Bias.* Retrieved from https://www.merriam-webster.com/dictionary/bias

Merriam-Webster. (2018b). *Prejudice.* Retrieved from https://www.merriam-webster.com/dictionary/prejudice

Miller, K. (2016). *How to fight your own implicit biases.* Retrieved from https://www.aauw.org/2016/03/30/fight-your-biases/

MOOC List. (2017). *Diversity and inclusion in the workplace (Coursera).* Retrieved from https://www.mooc-list.com/tags

National Center for Education Statistics. (2018). *Concentration of public school students eligible for free or reduced-price lunch.* Retrieved from https://nces.ed.gov/programs/coe/indicator_clb.asp

Ogden, J. (2016). Are you in need of bibliotherapy? *Psychology Today.* Retrieved from https://www.psychologytoday.com/us/blog/trouble-in-mind/201602/are-you-in-need-bibliotherapy

Parent Teacher Home Visits. (2016). *PTHV model.* Retrieved from http://www.pthvp.org/what-we-do/pthv-model/

Rinderle, S. (2018). *Think you need cultural sensitivity training? Think again.* Retrieved from https://www.workforce.com/2018/05/10/think-need-cultural-sensitivity-training-think/

Southern Poverty Law Center. (2018). *Teaching Tolerance Webinars.* Retrieved from https://www.tolerance.org/professional-development/webinars

Statista. (2018). *K-12 public school enrollment numbers in the United States from 2000-2013, by ethnicity (in 1,000).* Retrieved from https://www.statista.com/statistics/236238/us-public-school-enrollment-by-ethnicity/

Suttie, J. (2016). *Four ways teachers can reduce implicit bias.* Retrieved from https://greatergood.berkeley.edu/article/item/four_ways_teachers_can_reduce_implicit_bias Tennyson. (n.d.a). *About.* Retrieved from http://sarahtennyson.com/about/

Tennyson. (n.d.b). *Is unconscious bias limiting your success as a mentor?* Retrieved from http://sarahtennyson.com/is-unconscious-bias-limiting-your-success-as-a-mentor/

The National SEED Project. *About SEED.* Retrieved from https://nationalseedproject.org/about-us/about-seed

Walker, T. (2018). Who is the average U.S. teacher? *neaToday.* Retrieved from http://neatoday.org/2018/06/08/who-is-the-average-u-s-teacher/

Wolz, J. (2017). *Why teachers should travel.* Retrieved from http://teacheroffduty.com/why-teachers-should-travel

About the Primary Authors

Nicholas D. Young, PhD, EdD

Dr. Nicholas D. Young has worked in diverse educational roles for more than 30 years, serving as a teacher, counselor, principal, special education director, graduate professor, graduate program director, graduate dean, and longtime psychologist and superintendent of schools. He was named the Massachusetts Superintendent of the Year; and he completed a distinguished Fulbright program focused on the Japanese educational system through the collegiate level. Dr. Young is the recipient of numerous other honors and recognitions including the General Douglas MacArthur Award for distinguished civilian and military leadership and the Vice Admiral John T. Hayward Award for exemplary scholarship. He holds several graduate degrees including a PhD in educational administration and an EdD in educational psychology.

Dr. Young has served in the U.S. Army and U.S. Army Reserves combined for over 34 years; and he graduated with distinction from the U.S. Air War College, the U.S. Army War College, and the U.S. Navy War College. After completing a series of senior leadership assignments in the U.S. Army Reserves as the commanding officer of the 287th Medical Company (DS), the 405th Area Support Company (DS), the 405th Combat Support Hospital, and the 399th Combat Support Hospital, he transitioned to his current military position as a faculty instructor at the U.S. Army War College in Carlisle, PA. He currently holds the rank of Colonel.

Dr. Young is also a regular presenter at state, national, and international conferences; and he has written many books, book chapters, and/or articles on various topics in education, counseling, and psychology. Some of his most recent books include *Sounding the Alarm in the Schoolhouse: Safety, Security and Student Well-Being (2019); Creating Compassionate Classrooms: Understanding the Continuum of Disabilities and Effective Educational Interventions* (2019); *The Special Education Toolbox: Supporting Exceptional Teachers, Students, and Families* (in-press); *Acceptance, Understanding, and the Moral Imperative of Promoting Social Justice Education in the Schoolhouse* (in-press); *Educating the Experienced: Challenges and Best Practices in Adult Learning* (in-press); *Securing the Schoolyard: Protocols that*

Promote Safety and Positive Student Behaviors (2018); *The Soul of the Schoolhouse: Cultivating Student Engagement* (2018); *Embracing and Educating the Autistic Child: Valuing Those Who Color Outside the Lines* (2018); *From Cradle to Classroom: A Guide to Special Education for Young Children* (2018); *Captivating Classrooms: Educational Strategies to Enhance Student Engagement* (2018); *Potency of the Principalship: Action-Oriented Leadership at the Heart of School Improvement* (2018); *Soothing the Soul: Pursuing a Life of Abundance Through a Practice of Gratitude* (2018); *Dog Tags to Diploma: Understanding and Addressing the Educational Needs of Veterans, Servicemembers, and their Families* (2018); *Turbulent Times: Confronting Challenges in Emerging Adulthood* (2018); *Guardians of the Next Generation: Igniting the Passion for Quality Teaching* (2018); *Achieving Results: Maximizing Success in the Schoolhouse* (2018); *From Head to Heart: High Quality Teaching Practices in the Spotlight* (2018); *Stars in the Schoolhouse: Teaching Practices and Approaches that Make a Difference* (2018); *Making the Grade: Promoting Positive Outcomes for Students with Learning Disabilities* (2018); *Paving the Pathway for Educational Success: Effective Classroom Interventions for Students with Learning Disabilities* (2018); *Wrestling with Writing: Effective Strategies for Struggling Students* (2018); *Floundering to Fluent: Reaching and Teaching the Struggling Student* (2018); *Emotions and Education: Promoting Positive Mental Health in Students with Learning* (2018); *From Lecture Hall to Laptop: Opportunities, Challenges, and the Continuing Evolution of Virtual Learning in Higher Education* (2017); *The Power of the Professoriate: Demands, Challenges, and Opportunities in 21st Century Higher Education* (2017); *To Campus with Confidence: Supporting a Successful Transition to College for Students with Learning Disabilities* (2017); *Educational Entrepreneurship: Promoting Public-Private Partnerships for the 21st Century* (2015); *Beyond the Bedtime Story: Promoting Reading Development during the Middle School Years* (2015); *Betwixt and Between: Understanding and Meeting the Social and Emotional Developmental Needs of Students During the Middle School Transition Years* (2014); *Learning Style Perspectives: Impact Upon the Classroom* (3rd ed., 2014); and *Collapsing Educational Boundaries from Preschool to PhD: Building Bridges Across the Educational Spectrum* (2013); *Transforming Special Education Practices: A Primer for School Administrators and Policy Makers* (2012); and *Powerful Partners in Student Success: Schools, Families and Communities* (2012). He also co-authored several children's books to include the popular series *I am Full of Possibilities*. Dr. Young may be contacted directly at nyoung1191@aol.com.

Elizabeth Jean, EdD

Dr. Elizabeth Jean has served as an elementary school educator and administrator in various rural and urban settings in Massachusetts for more than 20 years. As a building administrator, she has fostered partnerships with staff, families, various local businesses, and higher education institutions. Further, she is currently a graduate adjunct professor at the Van Loan School of Education, Endicott College and previously taught at the College of Our Lady of the Elms. In terms of formal education, Dr. Jean received a BS in education from Springfield College; an MEd in education with a concentration in reading from the College of Our Lady of the Elms; and an EdD in curriculum, teaching, learning and leadership from Northeastern University.

Dr. Jean is a primary author on *Acceptance, Understanding, and the Moral Imperative of Promoting Social Justice Education in the Schoolhouse* (in-press); *From Cradle to Classroom: A Guide to Special Education for Young Children* (2019); *The Potency of the Principalship: Action-Oriented Leadership at the Heart of School Improvement* (2018); *Dog Tags to Diploma: Understanding and Addressing the Educational Needs of Veterans, Servicemembers and their Families* (2018); *Stars in the Schoolhouse: Teaching Practices and Approaches that Make a Difference* (2018); *From Head to Heart: High Quality Teaching Practices in the Spotlight* (2018); *From Lecture Hall to Laptop: Opportunities, Challenges and the Continuing Evolution of Virtual Learning in Higher Education* (2017). She has also written book chapters on such topics as emotional well-being for students with learning disabilities, post-secondary campus supports for emerging adults, parental supports for students with learning disabilities, home-school partnerships, virtual education, public and private partnerships in public education, professorial pursuits, technology partnerships between K-12 and higher education, developing a strategic mindset for LD students, the importance of skill and will in developing reading habits for young children, and middle school reading interventions to name a few. Additionally, she has co-authored and illustrated several children's books to include *Yes, Mama* (2018), *The Adventures of Scotty the Skunk: What's that Smell?* (2014), and the *I am Full of Possibilities* Series for Learning Disabilities Worldwide. She may be contacted at elizabethjean1221@gmail.com.

Teresa Allissa Citro, PhD

Dr. Citro is the Chief Executive Officer, Learning Disabilities Worldwide, Inc. and the Founder and President of Thread of Hope, Inc. She is a graduate of Tufts New England Medical School and Northeastern

University, Boston. Dr. Citro has co-edited several books on a wide range of topics in special education and she co-authored a popular children's series *I Am Full of Possibilities*. She is the co-editor of two peer review journals including *Learning Disabilities: A Contemporary Journal and Insights on Learning Disabilities* from *Prevailing Theories to Validated Practices*. She is the mother of two beautiful children and resides in New England.

www.ingramcontent.com/pod-product-compliance
Lightning Source LLC
Chambersburg PA
CBHW061844300426
44115CB00013B/2494